AMBRA | V

Accountability Technologies Tools for Asking Hard Questions

Dietmar Offenhuber, Katja Schechtner (Eds.)

AMBRA |V

Editors

Dietmar Offenhuber
Katja Schechtner

afo architekturforum oberösterreich
Herbert-Bayer-Platz 1
A-4020 Linz
www.afo.at

© 2013 AMBRA |V
AMBRA |V is part of Medecco Holding GmbH, Vienna
Printed in Austria

Cover Design and Typesetting: Gertrude Plöchl
Cover Image: Visualization of the annotated Guttenberg
dissertation (section) kindly provided by GuttenPlag - User8
under the Creative Commons license
http://de.guttenplag.wikia.com/wiki/Thumbnail
Photo Editing: Christian Schepe
Concept and Editing: Gabriele Kaiser
Proofreading and Copy Editing: Brian Dorsey
Printing and Binding: Gutenberg-Werbering GmbH, A-Linz
Printed on acid-free and chlorine-free bleached paper

printed climate-neutrally O CP IKS-Nr.: 53401-1307-1002

With 42 colored and 4 black-and-white figures

ISBN 978-3-99043-539-7 AMBRA |V

Preface

The basic need of civil society to live in responsibly planned and managed cities, to be involved in the planning process, or to at least be informed about it, has become a renewed focal point of debate in the past years.

While the incipient criticism of the institutionalized and oft-unquestioned decision-making chain of urban planning was accompanied by a basic struggle for more say and participation in the 1970s, the varieties of participation, the technical possibilities of knowledge transfer and the understanding of transparency—keyword Open Data—have fundamentally changed in today's information society. Much suggests that the classic distribution of roles between public and "individual" responsibility and the interface between citizens, activists and government have to be re-negotiated under new conditions.

With the help of visualization, analysis and measurement tools subsumed under the term *Accountability Technologies*, as well as socio-cultural practices, extensive data on noise, environmental pollution, mobility and corruption, for instance, can be compiled and represented. This book exemplarily shows which socio-political areas of action are opened up by *Accountability Technologies*, but also which critical aspects are tied in with them. Such as, for example, the seemingly simple insight that the enormous convolutes of availably-made data are neither neutral, nor do they imply a better understanding of complex processes "per se." The subtitle of this book indicates the direction: *Accountability Technologies* are to be understood as *Tools for Asking Hard Questions*, not as keys to ultimate answers.

Like the volume *Inscribing a Square: Urban Data as Public Space* (Springer Verlag, 2012), edited by Katja Schechtner and Dietmar Offenhuber as well, this publication also rests upon the precondition that architecture and urbanism go far beyond the physical space and the singularity of built structure. The basis for this book is provided by the second edition of the symposium *Sensing Place/Placing Sense*, again carried out with exceptional cooperation between the AIT Austrian Institute of Technology, the Ars Electronica and the afo architekturforum oberösterreich within the scope of the Ars Electronica Festival 2012.

Thanks to these initiatives at the interface of several disciplines, the increasingly dense interweaving of urban data and their physical context has been continued in such an exciting way under the aspect of *Accountability Technologies*. I would like to thank all those involved, especially the two editors, for their competence and commitment in realizing this book.

What began as a one-off publication now reveals itself—also in its graphic appearance—as a mutually related, mutually stimulating twosome.

Gabriele Kaiser
afo architekturforum oberösterreich

CONTENTS

Protocols for Asking Hard Questions

Dietmar Offenhuber, Katja Schechtner

A growing part of the general public is concerned that cities are planned and governed in a responsible way. Accountability technologies stand for new, innovative approaches to make sure that urban governments and players who make decisions that affect the public are held accountable for their actions.

In the contemporary information society, the democratic obligation of the citizens to rigorously inform themselves so that they can participate in public affairs has become almost impossible to fulfill. Rather than submitting to the opinions of self-proclaimed experts, citizens need new ways to make sense of what is going on around them. In this context, Michael Schudson coined the term of the "monitorial citizen," who "scans (rather than reads) the informational environment," ready to mobilize when alerted (Schudson, 1998).

And citizens indeed have questions about where their trash goes, about the air quality in their neighborhood, or whether their streets are well-managed. The past few years saw an emergence of practices dedicated to such concerns. This volume collects recent examples of these practices, including citizen sensing of environmental pollution, investigative data journalism revealing corruption, or crowd-sourced initiatives for social action. We were interested in projects that actually made an impact on the reality of the city in order to learn from them. We were interested in the motivations, strategies and tactics of the people who create and use these technologies. We were also interested in the role of representation—does it make a difference how information is presented?

We use the term "accountability technologies" for a collection of different tools and practices that are sometimes used in combination, sometimes separately. These practices include, but are not limited to citizen science projects, for example, to collect environmental data using DIY sensing technologies; Open Data and transparency initiatives for making urban planning and governance more transparent; initiatives for documenting the misuse of power or corruption using whistleblower platforms or online video websites; social visualization tools deeply integrated into online media formats, recently termed "data journalism" and, finally, advocacy tools for maximizing the impact of initiatives. More broadly, accountability technologies are concerned with three different aspects: the collection and generation of data, the analysis and dissemination of this data, and, lastly, its strategic use in the public discourse, in the legal system or political processes. Ultimately, accountability technologies are tools allowing citizens to challenge the authority of political elites, as well as tools for public administrations to engage the public in a discourse on shared issues.

However, the ways in which accountability technologies can have an impact in the public sphere are manifold and often convoluted, matching the ambiguity of the term "accountability" itself (Schedler, Diamond and Plattner, 1999, pp. 13–28). One meaning of the term is narrative, often circumscribed as answerability: It requires someone who makes decisions to offer a rational explanation of these decisions. The second meaning is related to enforcement, meaning the presence of instruments to make sure that the one who makes decisions maintains some responsibility for their consequences. Both meanings of accountability depend on a functioning democratic system that honors both justification and responsibility. Accountability technologies rely on a cooperative relationship between the individual and the government, since these technologies interface with mechanisms that need to be, at least in principle, already built into the system. The notion of accountability acknowledges the fact that full transparency is not possible where humans make decisions, and is probably also not desirable, since it would make it very difficult to make any decisions at all. The

technologies and practices discussed in this symposium operate at this interface between the citizens, activists and the government, tackling the question of how public
responsibility and democratic participation can happen in an information-saturated
society.

This volume is structured in three sections, corresponding to the main aspects of
successful social accountability campaigns which we term "collect," "comprehend"
and "compel." The first aspect deals with the question of how to collect a solid body
of data and evidence that withstands scrutiny. When enough data is available, the
challenge becomes making sense of it, extracting the gist and communicating it in an
effective way. The final aspect is how these insights can be put into action, by using
legal instruments, forging coalitions, creating public pressure and shaping new institutional mechanisms.

Collect

The artists **Amber Frid-Jimenz and Ben Dalton** address the embedded politics of big data
and critique the implicit assumption of data being neutral and objective. They discuss
an array of approaches for data scientists, artists and designers to counteract what
they call "unaccountability," or practices aimed at evading accountability. The citizen
science and DIY initiative **Public Lab** presents a striking example of the power of community-led civic science projects that transform the use of technology and interaction
with authorities. Similar to Frid-Jimenez and Dalton, the essay argues for opening
methodologies to integrate traditional scientific methods, institutional critique from
the arts and participative practices to create a data-literate public. **Sarah Williams**
presents a case study of air quality monitoring in Beijing during the 2008 Summer
Olympics. Williams and her team enlisted members of the international press corps
to measure the air quality during the events, using state-of-the-art environmental sensors. The visual comparison of the measured levels with other cities, such as New
York City or London, was just as important for communicating with the public as
collecting the data itself. **Dietmar Offenhuber**'s essay differentiates the oft-conflated concepts of transparency and accountability, and addresses some of the downsides and
limits of social accountability and community-led initiatives.

Comprehend

While mediated and crowd-sourced data collection strategies are in many ways new
to institutions and the public, they constitute only a small part compared to the vast
archives of institutional records that have been created for accountability purposes,
including birth records, statistical yearbooks of various public authorities and newspaper archives. The second part of the book examines new approaches to collaboratively analyzing both historical and current data sets and investigates how authorities,
media and individual activists inscribe meaning into data.

Pablo Rey Mazón presents a visualization approach aimed at exploring how newspapers tell and make stories. His tool allows the literal "coverage" of specific issues
on newspaper front pages to be analyzed over time, and juxtaposes this coverage
with information from social media. Visualization tools for corporate accountability
are the focus of the designer **Leonardo Bonanni**. His project, *sourcemap.com*, provides
an online mapping platform for investigating and visualizing the global supply chains
of consumer products. His platform, which is not only used by citizens, but also within
companies, is aimed at those "internal activists" who are willing to instigate change
from within companies and institutions. **Dieter Zinnbauer** offers the novel concept of
"Ambient Accountability" for fighting everyday corruption and raising awareness at

Ina Schieferdecker, Jeffery Warren, Amber Frid Jimenez; Michael Kreil, Dietmar Offenhuber
Symposium *Sensing Place / Placing Sense* II at the afo architectureforum upper austria as part of the Ars Electronica Festival 2012

the micro-level. He presents models for physical interventions that can bridge the gap between expectations, norms, information and accountability in the face of corrupt practices or institutional underperformance. Finally, **Lawrence Lessig** explains the components and implications of what he calls a political "read-write culture," the shift of political campaigning from a centralized and heavily choreographed model to a decentralized one. Following the "logic of collective action," which favors powerful minorities, Lessig also addresses the limits of institutional transparency mechanisms.

Compel

The last section explores how the "powers that be" can be persuaded or forced into action, and how institutions respond to the changing landscapes of interaction and communication between authorities and citizens.

The anonymous authors behind the pseudonym **PlagDoc** provide insight into the inner workings of one of the most spectacular successes of investigative crowdsourcing: the meticulous collaborative reconstruction and verification of numerous instances of plagiarism in the dissertation of the former German Secretary of Defense, which led to the resignation of the once-popular politician. The urban planning scholar and activist **Aaron Naparstek** tells the story of success and failure of the *Uncivil Servants* platform, a citizen initiative targeting the misuse of police parking permits in New York City. He shows how difficult it can be to hold individuals within an institution accountable—especially if the self-monitorial procedures of the organization are weak and internal activists for change face repercussions from their colleagues. The technologist and DIY enthusiast **Tomás Diez** explains the significance of *Fab Labs* and a DIY culture for fostering civic discourse between citizens and their city, using the example of Barcelona's new infrastructure of spaces where citizens can use and co-develop technologies for environmental sensing. **Katja Schechtner** explores the links between internal activists and the different models multi-lateral institutions, national and municipal governments pursue to tap into the expertise of their citizenry. Finally, discussing his work in the area of crisis mapping and digital activism, **Patrick Meier** describes how he and his group of tech-savvy volunteers first challenged the self-image of professional humanitarians as being superior domain experts in times of crisis and how the United Nations found ways to integrate their hierarchical procedures with the decentralized, horizontal approaches of the *Standby Volunteer Task Force*.

Acknowledgements

This book is a second in a series about *Sensing Place/Placing Sense*—an adventure we started three years ago to examine theoretical and practical interventions on how we perceive, make sense of and interact with our cities. We are deeply grateful for the continuous guidance, support and encouragement of friends, fellow researchers artists and collaborators in various institutions, without whom we would never have been able to follow through.

Sami Ben Gharbia, Marek Tuszynski; Michel Reimon, Katja Schechtner, Tomás Diez, Dieter Zinnbauer
Photos: afo/Linde Klement, Gabriele Kaiser

First and foremost to Gabriele Kaiser, without whom the publication of our work would not have been possible: She not only hosted the symposiums and exhibitions at afo, the architectureforum upperaustria that frame our discussions, shared her extensive knowledge about publishing with us, coordinated with language editors, graphic designers and publishers, but also pushed us forward and still has not given up on us as friends. Danke!

We also thank the team that has now worked with us for the second time: Brian Dorsey, Gertrude Plöchl and our publishing editor, David Marold, as well as Angelika Heller from Ambra publishing. Moreover, Ewald Elmecker, Linde Klement and Karin Tausz supported us during the symposium with their know-how and talent in handling a diverse set of speakers, artists and a lively and engaged audience that stimulated the discussion about many issues concerning the context and practice of accountability technologies that we have included in the book.

We also thank Gerfried Stocker for welcoming us into the Ars Electronica community, the Austrian Institute of Technology (AIT) for supporting us in exploring new frontiers, and our friends Christian Kral, Henriette Spyra, Dietmar Bauer and Wojciech Czaja for insights, encouragement and compassionate listening.

Finally, we want to thank all of the speakers, scholars and artists who contributed their time, work and expertise: José-Luis de Vicente, Dieter Zinnbauer, Michel Reimon, Michael Kreil, Jeffrey Warren, Amber Frid-Jimenez, Ina Schieferdecker, Sami Ben Gharbia, Marek Tuszynski, Ben Dalton, Leonardo Bonanni, Pablo Rey Mazón, Sarah Williams, Lawrence Lessig, PlagDoc, Aaron Naparstek, Tomás Diez, Patrick Meier, Shannon Dosemagen, Matthew Lippincott, Liz Berry, Don Blair and Jessica Breen.

References

Schedler, Andreas; Diamond, Lawrence and Plattner, Marc F. (1999). *The Self-Restraining State: Power and Accountability in New Democracies*. Boulder, CO: Lynne Rienner Publishers.

Schudson, Michael (1998). "Changing Concepts of Democracy." In *MIT Communications Forum*. Cambridge, MA. http://web.mit.edu/comm-forum/papers/schudson.html.

COLLECT

Data Is Political: Investigation, Emotion and the Accountability of Institutional Critique

Amber Frid-Jimenez, Ben Dalton

Introduction

Analysts speculate about the impact of big data on international business and government policies. Meanwhile, proportionally few designers and artists have yet to take up the challenging questions of how large-scale digital information systems will reshape our future. A small but growing community of technically savvy designers and activists are leading the charge, raising aesthetic and political questions on the perception, use and sometimes misuse of data—questions traditionally left to science, journalism, and politics. Despite the efforts of a growing few, the need for more designers and artists to keep pace with the rate of technological innovation remains no less urgent. By bringing artists and designers together with data scientists and policymakers within the larger project of *Data Is Political*, we catalyse debate about the role of design and art to produce meaning through the presentation and analysis of big data.[1] Our goal for this chapter is to lay the foundation and vocabulary on which that discussion builds and accountability is maintained.

We use the term "big data" to refer to enormous-scale data storage, processing and connectedness, often on global scales. Digital information systems have reduced the cost of copying and connecting cultural, scientific and social signals. In contrast to the high production costs of analogue copies, once digitised, all kinds of archives from early movies, to rooftop radiation sensor streams, to political voting records are reduced to signals that can be duplicated and transferred fluidly across our global internetwork at a relatively low cost and without the slightest degradation. Designers and artists use these digital signals to remap the original data into new forms in service of creating new meanings. In the contemporary data-saturated context, the process of remapping signals from colour to sound, from percentages to spatial plots, from individual images to curated stories, becomes as effortless as dragging-and-dropping bits or writing code commands.

Key technological breakthroughs in computation over the last century precede the current ease with which we produce, present and distribute data. By 1948, Claude Shannon's information theory had proven mathematically that digitised files could remain perfect copies through repeated processing and global transmission (Shannon, 1948). Our current modes of production take advantage of the rapid rate of duplication and sharability that Shannon's theory affords. Moore's Law, which describes the doubling of transistors on circuits every two years, has characterised the acceleration of storage and networking technology, reflecting the ongoing trend of rapid information infrastructure growth from the invention of the integrated circuit in 1958 onwards.

Despite these key innovations, working with data was, until recently, an elite activity. The technology required to capture and re-edit film, or to collect and map weather data was out of reach for all but a few well-funded scientists, commercial entertainers, advertisers and military researchers. Information processing tasks were expensive and required specialised training. A politics of scarcity limited the need for large-scale accountability. We define "accountability" in this context to mean an obligation to clearly demonstrate the methods by which data are collected, processed, used, presented and distributed. Until data processing moved off university computers and into the public around 1999, identifying who was collecting and using which data and how was relatively easy because the community of researchers who had access was small enough to monitor themselves.[2] However, as the tools of digital copying continue to reduce in cost, more and more people and organisations have access to larger and larger data sets, calling for an evaluation of modes and practices of accountability.

The scientific community has long worked with data representation, establishing widely accepted conventions of accountability, including open data, reproducibility, peer review and explicit statements of uncertainty. Recently, designers have been called upon to work on interfaces that represent or are driven by huge data sets. However, in large part, designers have not been trained in scientific or statistical data conventions, and so often have not considered how their design choices, such as which filters, visual shapes and simplifications to use, affect meaning and application. The reach of big data and big processing is making a much wider group of people, including graphic designers and artists, into data scientists without them necessarily realising it. The creative potential of this new situation is boundless, and necessitates the development of new conventions of accountability for data-driven design practices.

Traditionally, data has been used to hold people accountable for their actions, identifying hidden connections, corroborating stories, providing evidence and proving theories. In this sense, data remapping and visualisation has always been a technique of accountability. But data are also used for many other reasons now—to connect us, evince emotion and mediate our experience of each other and the world. Artists and designers engaging with data provide new possibilities for storytelling and communication, but must also keep in mind that as this artistic field grows, data resources grow even faster, and so, too, the power of the people that own them. Creative practitioners should focus attention equally on designing new accountability tools, recognising that companies with big data centres and infrastructure continue to manage and restrict access, even as we design more tools for data accountability. Our responsibility then is to question the limits of current accountability tools, providing new techniques and interfaces to ask how (and where) data resources are managed.

In this chapter we describe data visualisation and other forms of art and design working with data as a process of remapping. We define three axes of data remapping: *investigative design*, *emotive reframing* and *institutional critique*, on which we lay out the implications of big data on design practice. Reviewing the full potential of tools for accountability requires us to imagine them being used on our behalf as well as against us. We analyse the role of big data in accountability by examining both its potential benefits and its uses as a means of *unaccountability*, or evading practices of accountability. We conclude by exploring strategies to design out unaccountability, arguing for the potential of principles of openness to guarantee access and use of big data accountability tools.

Axes of Remapping

It's important to realize that visualization is a medium. You are framing your argument all the way from how you gather your data, to how you curate it, to what comes out ... you are framing reality.—Fernanda Viegas[3]

Our understanding of the potential uses of big data within accountability technologies is grounded in a history of exemplars. However, the significant examples of data remapping were developed at a time when only comparatively small data sets were technically possible. The potential of big data tools is still largely untested, and represents a significant space for exploration by artists, designers and data scientists. Many data scientists and designers we spoke to within the last year as a part of the *Data Is Political* project testified to the need for testing, discourse and convention within this relatively new territory. Philip DeCamp, data scientist from the Cognitive Machines Group at the MIT Media Lab, described his process:

As you start dealing with more complex visualisations shoving together multi-modal sets and adding a bunch of camera movements and scripted events, you have to make a lot of design choices. If you're looking at new kinds of data, there is no convention; you just have to make things up.

On one hand, the artistic freedom DeCamp describes is tantalising for applied artists who dream of fewer constraints on their work, but, on the other, indicates the need for a deep examination of how certain design decisions affect meaning.

The term "data visualisation" often describes contemporary tools and techniques of storytelling with data. We find it unsatisfying in its implied limitation to the visual, proposing instead a definition that includes many overlapping forms from different fields and perspectives. Our conversations have yielded descriptions of data visualisation ranging from a single, personalised sentence summarising political news, to spatial and auditory systems, to tools for interrogating the visual effect of filtering world health data sets as a means to provide evidence to policymakers. From this breadth, we define the three axes of remapping outlined below.

Investigative Design

Investigative design is grounded in a history of visual language for statistical analysis and scientific investigation. Although not constrained solely to visual media, the definition of "graphical excellence" from Edward Tufte characterises the objectives of investigative design well, as complex data communicated with "clarity, precision and efficiency" (Tufte, 1983, p. 51). Tufte's intention is to enable an audience to ask questions of complex systems with a minimum of distortion and distraction in the design elements. As the speed increases with which data can be collected and processed, we expect greater levels of investigative design within journalism. The *New York Times*, for example, have dedicated "graphics editors" who work with data and visualisation in their journalism.

> The goal is still to see how I can help guide my reader, how I can explain something … The reporter writes a sentence, and then the supporting evidence is the quote below it. We write a sentence and the supporting evidence is the chart below it. — Amanda Cox

Design that provokes questions enhances accountability within complex systems, making clear ties in networks that previously have been hard or impossible to see.

Emotive Reframing

Whereas investigative designs often have specific tasks of understanding as a core motivation, emotive reframing images tend to be focused more on persuasion. Emotive reframing in design resonates with someone through poetic analogy or experience. Although not always the case, reducing the functional efficiency of investigative design often can heighten emotive reframing. A distinct authorial voice defines the aesthetic and narrative aspects of this type of practice. Media theorist and activist Florian Schneider uses the analogy of framing, an act traditionally used in photography and conceptual art practices, to describe how this mode of data-driven design functions:

> This moment of framing tells us more about the desire to establish a relationship rather than about reality itself.

The degree of reframing can vary from close correlation to abstract representation. A single emotive image can be used to represent an entire data set. For instance, Casey Reas described the example of abstracting out the analysis of climate science data on

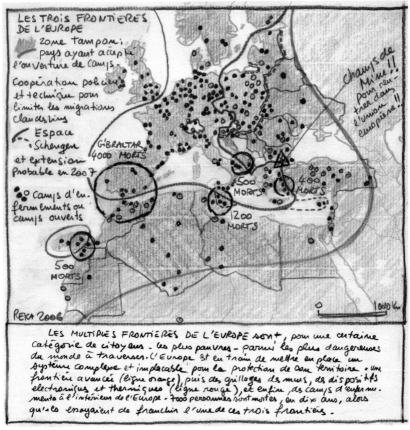

Les Trois Frontières de l'Europe, original map: Philippe Rekacewicz, 2006

gradual warming to an image of a polar bear on a melting ice flow. In this example, the photograph acts as a hook, communicating the issue through the immediacy of a single image without the need to spend time interpreting analytical details. However, to remain part of the data visualisation process, emotive reframing must link back to more detailed investigative design or discussion.

Combining emotive and investigative dimensions in a single design is a challenging balance of storytelling and interrogation. Philippe Rekacewicz, radical cartographer and journalist for *Le Monde diplomatique*, combines emotional impact with the precision of traditional map making. Many of Philippe's maps are hand-drawn, an approach that captures the human stories of the underlying data, whilst at the same time acknowledging his own authorial voice within the constraints of geographic mapping. For example, *Les Trois Frontières de l'Europe* maps immigration camps and the European frontiers to people seeking asylum (Rekacewicz, 2006). The map efficiently shows the infrastructure of migration and in that sense conforms successfully to cartographic convention. However, Rekacewicz's map goes beyond convention, using the uniqueness of a hand-crafted line to emphasise the humanity of the migration: The ambiguous borders of internment camps outside the Schengen Area are sketched in wider, less certain pencil line, and dominating black circles and blood-red type mark the brutality of the lives lost in perilous sea crossings. Design that reframes data to resonate emotionally with an audience has the potential to reach beyond already engaged groups to a wider population, bringing to light injustices and mobilising efforts to enforce accountability.

Institutional Critique

The axes of investigative design and emotive reframing capture most examples of visualisation. However, a third form of remapping data exists. This third axis measures the meta-analysis of the systems of data collection, processing and presentation themselves. Whilst traditional techniques, such as source citation and error bars expressing uncertainty, capture part of the overall frames of reference, assumptions and ideological underpinnings of data science, self-criticality is lacking from many examples of investigative design.

Artists have been interrogating the use of materials, as well as critiquing institutional organisations for a long time. We can therefore draw key examples of institutional critique in data analysis from art history. *MoMA Poll* by Hans Haacke is a classic example of institutional critique (1970). For the piece, Haacke placed a transparent voting box in the gallery to measure gallery audience opinion on MoMA donor and board member Governor Nelson Rockefeller's support for President Nixon's Indochina Policy in 1970. Due to the political controversy that the piece elicited, rumour has it that the day after the opening, the work came under the threat of removal. The artwork commented directly on the relationship between the gallery and global political systems, implicating Haacke himself, his curator and the institution in a web of political and social power structures. The threat of removal endangered the artist's livelihood, and constituted a clear and real form of self-critique and, by extension, institutional critique. Questioning assumptions and perspectives within a system brings fallacies to the surface and prevents people and organisations from being able to intentionally hide their motivations.

> Archives are far from neutral repositories of information. They have become vibrant sites for cultural production. The archive is no longer seen simply as a static form to be mined, but instead is vital for staging new agendas in politics.— Nomeda and Gediminas Urbonas

Unaccountability Technologies

The greatest challenge to accountability technology is not technical or aesthetic, but instead concerns the politics of accountability. There are many motivations to remain unaccountable. The dimensions of remapping described in the previous section each offer ways to be accountable and at the same time can be used to deflect or repress accountability. Greater storage, processing and connectedness motivate some people to use big data to create systems to block accountability, whilst calling others to action for the sake of holding those with power over the infrastructure accountable for their decisions and actions.

Designers are often employed to use their insights and skills in persuasion to the advantage of political and commercial ends. Investigative designers leverage the visual language established by science and journalism documentation because of its power for explanation and exploration. Often, established indicators of clarity and efficiency can be appropriated to lend a sense of authority or trust to misleading data. For example, the formality of graphs, maps and other typical visualisation techniques are often assumed to be inherently accountable. However, information used to create a design may have been fabricated, the underlying process may have been modified, or a distorting assumption may not have been made clear. As data size and processing complexity increase, audiences run the risk of becoming dependent on shorthand symbols of trust in place of taking the requisite time to investigate the sources and assumptions themselves.

> Because we usually deal with 'data' and 'numbers' people think that visualisation is a 'neutral' tool: 'Well, I'm just showing the numbers, it's the truth.'—Fernanda Viegas

Of the three axes of remapping that we have outlined, emotive reframing is the most dependent on the author's choices to ensure the connection between the underlying information and the story being told. This means that a skilled storyteller can easily use the techniques of emotional connection and persuasion to deliberately draw attention away from certain questions or ideas and toward others. With the advent of big data tools of profiling and real-time processing, personalisation can be used for unaccountability to adjust stories being told for each person individually, to match their prejudices, or to take advantage of their particular blind spots. In the remaining part of this chapter, we review the potential of design to support accountability through big data remapping, to resist or identify unaccountability, and to sustain tools of accountability in the face of complexity and opposition from those who do not stand to benefit from them.

Designing Out Unaccountability

Successfully balancing the axes of remapping creates design that is investigative, emotive and critical. Citation of sources, expression of uncertainty and critique of process are key features of effective data-driven design. The audience should be assisted in asking what range of possible meanings the source data suggest, about the fallibility of the narrator, and about the assumptions and simplifications that have been made. These general principles offer a framework to tackle unaccountability in big data systems and underpin guidelines for artists and designers who find themselves dealing with questions of data remapping without the context of traditional statistics or visualisation training. Data science, too, can grow more effective from this dialogue by borrowing institutional critique from the arts, and extending criticality beyond the current data analysis to include the broader system of funding, research direction and infrastructure resource. Furthermore, emotive reframing can be employed to reach wider audiences with greater impact.

Distinguishing between visualisation norms that infer symbolic trust and the accountability of an underlying data process requires a level of information design literacy.

> Giving people the literacy to understand is a key concern to us. It is part of the empowerment. If people are literate, and they understand how these things work, then that gives them the power. — Martin Wattenberg

Data literacy must attempt to keep pace with adapting forms of decoy and camouflage used to evoke a sense of trust without supporting analysis. When designed effectively and with an eye toward literacy, big data systems enable "training" examples to be added to many more facets of life. Experience at reading information design will develop as the tools to process and display data become more prevalent.

Digital display, along with associated connectedness and processing, allow for infinite layers of detail in a visualisation. In print design, finding space to show both an overview and a detailed story on a single page was a considerable challenge. Whilst the "no wasted ink" design principles are still a core aspect of investigative design, dimensions such as zoom, linked space, transparency, blur and time allow for complexity to be available to a viewer if needed. Interaction goes a long way towards displaying the effects of the assumptions and filters that have been applied.

> With the kind of data sets we are working with now, having a single result is very misleading ... you need to be able to compare multiple results, that's really where the information is ... in the ability to filter the data in different ways to reveal other possibilities. — Casey Reas

The viewer can play with the assumptions of a visualisation through interactivity in order to understand their effects. However, not everyone will have time or inclination to explore underlying processes in data remapping. Systems should record the reviews of those that do, so that people can rely on personal networks of trust.

Beyond systems that expose key parameters to interactive control are toolkits that enable entire processes of remapping to be explored. Growing ecosystems of computation, rendering libraries and tools are enabling designers, programmers and artists to build new forms of remapping. A trade-off must be struck between complexity of the interface and depth of possible exploration. Whilst such systems require significant training and experience to use, the number of people with access to this potential is much greater than during the time of data and processing scarcity. The number of data remapping designers will continue to grow as the community of experienced users continue to document their development and use of these tools. Free and open access, therefore, must be a requirement for software ecosystems of exploration, documentation and sharing of data remapping techniques.

A Race for Openness

Open data, open tools, open processes; without these, how can we audit the stories that are being told? Data collection, processing and remapping technologies should be, at a minimum, open source so that the assumptions used can be analysed. For incremental exploration and development of these tools, a free software license is also required, so that creators with significant resources do not retain control over what can and cannot be held accountable with those tools. Freedom to appropriate also decentralises the remapping process by removing a need to seek access or permission.

> The question of how [big data systems are] controlled becomes essentially the question of politics. The good news is that we've been working on this problem for several tens of thousands of years, and the downside is ... politics isn't a solved problem, and so the politics of data is not going to be a solved problem either.— Benjamin Mako Hill

The scale of big data systems presents new challenges to open access approaches to accountability. If a large corporation or government were to open up its archive for download, no one but other corporations and governments would have the resources to store and process it.

> Everything goes in the direction of opening data ... If there is no redistribution of infrastructure, it will sound great, but who is actually able to access that data?— Marcell Mars

Instead, in the current ecosystem of data infrastructure, individual users and small external organisations have to rely on the big data provider to maintain an "open API" (Application Programming Interface) for them to query parts of the data when they need them. Or people might use data analysis tools hosted by the big data provider to do their processing and remapping. The difficulty is that if tools rely on cloud services, they become dependent on or sustained by commercial interests. Controlled proprietary systems and limited APIs can shape what questions can be easily asked, or stories told. Using closed APIs limit how visualisations can be notated or augmented with alternative analysis.

Closed centralised information systems can lead to unaccountability and corruption when the actions and behaviour of the few people who control them are far from public view. Peter Sunde, co-founder of *The Pirate Bay*, points out the potential dangers of giving control to a concentrated few:

> All sorts of power corrupt people, so we should consider that when we build structures, that if you centralise things, corruption is possible.

Decentralisation, on the other hand, avoids concentrations of power that may lead to corruption. Indeed, open decentralised systems that put power in the hands of a multitude can engender accountability by their nature. However, decentralised systems are not free from other problems. Decentralising information can obfuscate the critical power structures underlying systems of governance. For example, recent neoliberal literature such as David Beito's *The Voluntary City* argues in favour of decentralising areas of government control, such as the oversight of the U.S. financial markets and environmental projection (Beito, Gordon, and Tabarrok, 2002). The ability to act freely, avoiding accountability in this case, is retained through a sleight of hand where a centralised objective is coordinated to retain unaccountable control of a seemingly distributed system. That is to say that distributing bits of information here and there in an uncoordinated way produces a signal-to-noise ratio that makes it difficult to analyse the whole system. A centralised information system, on the other hand, is perhaps easier to scrutinise from below as long as it is accessible. Whilst in this view centralised information systems seem to provide the potential for simple and effective accountability, adequate accessibility may be too difficult to guarantee. Decentralised systems can overcome this difficulty by deploying a diversity of system architecture and perspectives to strengthen independent accountability systems.

Big data infrastructures could potentially enable unconstrained critique and accountability of the big data corporations and government departments themselves. Decentralised systems offer one possible approach to this problem. The enormous library of popular culture stored and made accessible in BitTorrent ecosystems practically demonstrates the ability for big data storage distributed across the home computers of a large audience of users.

> What BitTorrent did for the internet was fundamentally amazing. It made computers servers again. It made computers converse with other computers.—Max Van Kleek

Projects like *WebBox* demonstrate the potential for distributed big data to offer "a new type of web where people can communicate with each other personally" (Van Kleek). Decentralised systems would be self-sustaining, once started, because much of the data held by big data corporations is currently collected from the work of the audience. For example, in a social network site the users add most of the value in analysing and documenting their social connections. Decentralised systems where an individual's data are stored in a distributed way across a network of other people's computers have been and still are technically possible. However, the weakness of decentralised systems of accountability is that any system can be "gamed", and the limits enforced to control this manipulation slow the effectiveness of the operation as a whole. Intentional system sabotage from coherent, centralised power is a significant threat. Moreover, the reasons why this kind of system does not compete with large-scale corporate cloud services are economic and political.

Those people and organisations who want to maintain unaccountability and who have vested interests in profiting from the work of the users within closed systems will resist a move towards open big data systems for accountability. In the face of such resistance, we need to identify, collate and critique attempts to derail progress towards further democratisation of data analysis and open systems of accountability. Making open systems that use big data to ensure accountability requires sustaining sufficient accountability in closed systems. This race condition produces an urgency to build open systems before the scale of data collected and processing available in closed systems is too great to compete with.

Building structures to document aspects of control in closed systems and openly cataloguing unaccountability technologies is imperative. This documentation must present dimensions of network connections, influence, ownership, physical resources and bottlenecks in the system. The three axes of remapping (investigative design, emotive reframing and institutional critique) offer a framework to enable artists, designers and data scientists to tackle the challenge of designing and building the open tools and systems necessary to maintain accountability and shape how big data will affect the way we communicate, share resources and live in the future.

References

Beito, David T.; Gordon, Peter and Tabarrok, Alexander (2002). *The Voluntary City: Choice, Community, and Civil Society*. Ann Arbor, MI: University of Michigan Press.

Haacke, Hans (1970). *MoMA Poll*. Installation. The Museum of Modern Art, New York.

Rekacewicz, Philippe (2006). "L'Europe et ses frontières paradoxales — Les blogs du Diplo." November 27. http://blog.mondediplo.net/2006-11-27-L-Europe-et-ses-frontieres-paradoxales

Shannon, Claude E. (1948). "A Mathematical Theory of Communication." *Bell System Technical Journal* 27 (October): pp. 379–423 and 623–656.

Tufte, Edward R. (1983). *The Visual Display of Quantitative Information*. Cheshire, CT: Graphics Press.

1 *Data Is Political* is a research project directed by the authors that investigates the aesthetics and politics of data, their collection, visualisation and distribution. The project explores the recent context of "big data" and its cultural implications for artists and designers. Big data is a term used to describe the expanding archives of digital information collected using the internet, mobile phones, surveillance cameras and other sensors in the environment. The project addresses the aesthetic and political dimensions of the contemporary condition that arises from an increased focus on collecting and presenting data. The project takes the form of interviews, symposia, projects, articles and a forthcoming book publication.

2 Distributed.net, launched in 1997, was the first system to enable a coordinated distributed data analysis task, but it wasn't until 1999 that the distributed method was popularised. The Space Sciences Laboratory at the University of California, Berkeley launched SETI@home (Search for Extra-Terrestrial Intelligence at home), allowing users to participate in a distributed computing task that analysed radio signals to search for signs of extra-terrestrial activity and intelligence.

3 All of the quotes in this chapter are taken from conversations recorded by the authors with artists, designers and data scientists, and from presentations at the *Data Is Political* symposium in Bergen. These perspectives were collected between 2011 and 2013. Available at: http://dataispolitical.net.

Civic, Citizen, and Grassroots Science:
Towards a Transformative Scientific Research Model

Public Lab

Shannon Dosemagen, Matthew Lippincott and Liz Barry (Public Laboratory for Open Technology and Science), Don Blair (Pioneer Valley Open Science), Jessica Breen (University of Kentucky, Geography)

All of the tools and practices highlighted in this volume focus on effective ways of investigating, drawing conclusions about, and making a convincing case to others regarding the state of the world. This process can roughly be categorized into three parts—*question formation, data collection,* and *interpretation*. Ultimately, these categories aren't very strict, and are always interwoven. Scientific research predominantly proceeds through a complex, iterative, nonlinear mix of hypothesis generation, data acquisition, and analysis; attempts to isolate "raw data," for example, inevitably require specifying a model of the world, and particular choices about what does and doesn't count as "legitimate" or "useful" data. In this chapter, we focus on the approach taken by Public Laboratory—both philosophically and through the lens of a particular case study and its creation of accountability and action for environmental engagement. We'll address the questions of: "*Why* is data being collected?" (*question formation*); "*How* is it being collected?" (*data collection*); and "*Who* is using the data?" (*interpretation*) by contrasting traditional, "certified scientists-only" research methods with emerging, more inclusive research methodologies, using the Public Lab's approach as an example. The case study examined in this chapter is Public Lab's second-longest running project, which addresses resident concerns about water quality and the cleanup process around the Gowanus Canal EPA Superfund Site in Brooklyn, New York. Launched in the winter of 2011, the project, *GLAM (Gowanus Low Altitude Mapping)* is in collaboration with the community groups Gowanus Canal Conservancy and the Gowanus Dredgers Canoe Club.

Public Laboratory for Open Technology and Science

The Public Laboratory for Open Technology and Science was established in the spring of 2010 when Gulf Coast residents, NGOs, and members of a growing online community, GrassrootsMapping.org, came together to collect over 100,000 aerial images of the Gulf Coast during the Deepwater Horizon disaster. Three of the Public Lab co-founders first came together during the spill in response to the ongoing media blackout and the difficulty coastal residents faced in accessing information about the cleanup process, ecological and public health, as well as the lack of opportunities to volunteer with spill cleanup efforts. Following the disaster, even local residents had difficulty gaining access to the area, and journalists were on some occasions actively prevented from visiting affected sites.

This was the first major project embarked on by the Public Lab community and it relied solely on low-cost and repurposed materials that were valued at under one hundred dollars. The goal of this project was to create a low-cost mechanism for grassroots community engagement and monitoring of the corporate and government response. Protected and stabilized in housings made from soda bottles, refurbished digital cameras were launched on kites and tethered balloons to between 500 and 2,000 feet to capture high-resolution aerial photos of the spill's effects. In 2011, Public Lab incorporated as a non-profit and has expanded its scope to include a wide range of environmental and social justice issues, facilitating a fully participatory, transformative form of civic science that is directed and owned by communities (Dosemagen et al., 2011).

Based on the initial promise of the *Grassroots Mapping* project and the "infectious" way that projects such as this spread (combining low-cost environmental technology with an open source license), Public Lab has been working on other novel and affordable research tools for investigating environmental health. These include a "do-it-yourself" (DIY) spectrometer that was initially developed to identify polyaromatic hydrocarbons (PAH) in soil and sediment, but has since been adapted to explore other goals such as testing of water samples, heavy metal contamination in soil and even emissions from smokestacks. Other tools in development include thermal "flashlights" for detecting thermal pollution, near-infrared cameras for examining vegetation health, indoor air toxic mapping of formaldehyde, and the repurposing of photographically sensitive paper strips for detecting hydrogen sulfide (H_2S) emissions near hydrofracking sites. In the 2 ½ years since the growing community started, Public Lab has expanded to articulate community-based participatory models of science-based environmental engagement, adapting and refining DIY research tools in a socially and politically aware context (Dosemagen et al., 2011).

Traditional, Grassroots, Civic and Citizen Science

Scientific research today is predominantly and, to some, definitionally conducted by professional scientists whose aim is to convince, through sanctioned, peer-reviewed channels, other members of their profession to accept hypotheses about the world—hypotheses that are often only comprehensible to a relatively small subset of the public. This state of affairs in which only a credentialed few are qualified to initiate, carry out, and interpret scientific studies has, in recent decades, been called into question both from within and from outside of the scientific establishment. Investigations of environmental toxics have faced criticism from statisticians questioning the validity of isolated investigative instances and from civic groups questioning the funding, motivation, and "situated engagement" of professional scientists (Ioannidis, 2005). The adoption in recent years of "crowd-sourced" data collection practices by professional scientists, as well as various initiatives in "civic science," "citizen science," and "grassroots science," all point to the emergence of alternative models for the production of scientific knowledge, practices that potentially open up research participation to those without conventional scientific credentials. These emerging practices present the possibility of science research which is more representative, accountable, and democratic in its goals and emphasis, and which, when combined with the fast-pace and low-cost innovations of an open source community, may result in more comprehensive and accurate data collection.

Modes of Participation in Research. In this new, increasingly open scientific landscape, it is useful to distinguish the various emerging modes and models of non-traditional scientific research through an analysis of the ways in which those *without* "scientific credentials" participate in official research activities: *who* is enabled to define question formation; *how* do credentialed and non-credentialed scientists collect data; *what* does credentialing mean for the quality and veracity of data; *for whose benefit* is interpretation conducted and conclusions drawn? To consider these questions is to ask how inclusive or exclusive current scientific research practices are and to suggest a framework for developing better research practices in the future. In what follows, we will apply a blend of analytical frameworks from communications and community organizing (Fuentes Batista, 2012) and *extreme citizen science* (Haklay, 2012) in order to begin to distinguish various levels of participation of "non-credentialed" individuals (i.e., those who are not "professional scientists") in scientific research programs.

Traditional Scientific Practice. Traditional, institutional scientific practice requires that those who wish to participate in all aspects of scientific research—*question formation*, *research funding*, *data collection*, and *access to and interpretation of results*—possess recognized credentials: a Master's degree, a doctorate, or other institutional certification. A prime example of this "by scientists, for scientists" approach is the publication of scientific journals, access to which is often limited to individuals formally associated with academic or research institutions which pay for subscriptions to these journals. This practice creates a hierarchy of access even amongst academic and research institutions as the subscriptions to these journals can cost thousands of dollars. Slightly greater inclusion is achieved when research data and interpretation are made available to the non-credentialed public, in various forms such as open access publishing and science journalism. Following Fuentes Batista (2012), we term this minimal level of inclusion *nominal* participation.

Crowdsourcing. Though the term is recent, "crowdsourcing," or the use of large numbers of volunteers to collect data for scientific research, is not. It has been used in the United States in one form or another since the late 1800s, starting with data collection efforts led by the National Weather Service (Clark and Illman, 2001). The rise of such practices in scientific research has allowed for increased public participation in traditional research projects. While projects labeled "crowd-sourced" include a rather diverse range of practices, in most, participants are given small incentives (monetary, social, or entertainment) in order to carry out relatively low-skill data collection tasks. The initiators of the research program, and the ultimate interpretation of the data, remain squarely the province of professional, credentialed scientists, who typically implement "crowd-sourced" techniques in order to enhance the scale and efficiency of the data collection process while keeping research costs low. This "citizens-as-sensors" (Goodchild, 2007) approach to collecting volunteer geographic information (VGI) is a form of *instrumental* participation in scientific research. Participants are treated as an apparatus who need not be aware of the implications of, or motivations for, the research data they are helping to collect, and are typically not cited for their contributions as partners in the research they helped to conduct.

Some applications of crowdsourcing allow participants to determine the particular mode in which they contribute to a pre-defined research agenda. For example, certain technological challenges or scientific problems might be posted on a website, and innovative solutions are then solicited from the general public. This increased level of participation might be deemed *representative*, in that participants are often recognized as individuals with significant contributions to the results of the research program, and are allowed to make decisions as to what types of tools or resources, usually within a pre-specified domain, might best be employed to pursue the research agenda in question. One example of this mode of participation is NASA's recent *CLOUDS* project (Crowdsourcing.org, 2012).

Civic, Citizen and Grassroots Science. Yet greater levels of inclusion are found in projects labeled "citizen," or "civic" science. Though numerous definitions of "citizen science" and "civic science" have been used (Clark and Illman, 2001; Fortun and Fortun, 2005; Cooper et al., 2007; Cohn, 2008; Bonney et al., 2009; Silverton, 2009; Dickenson et al., 2012), many of the projects placed in this category share a focus on including non-credentialed participants in research idea generation, implementation, and interpretation. To varying extents, such programs are conceived by individuals or groups who are engaged in using scientific methods to address questions about their *own* environment, or to invent or apply technology that solves a problem which *they* *themselves* face. Muki Haklay of the Extreme Citizen Science Laboratory at University College London has explained participation in citizen science in terms of four distinct levels (Haklay, 2012). Level one of Haklay's hierarchy is *crowdsourcing*, where citizens are used as a physical resource. The second level expands to the use of citizens as a cognitive resource in what Haklay calls *distributed intelligence*. The third level, *participatory science*, goes beyond simple data collection to include the involvement of citizens in defining the problem, with the fourth level, *extreme citizen science* expanding to include analysis of data. The greatest levels of inclusion on this end of the "participation spectrum" involve individuals for whom the incentive to participate arises from a directly perceived need, or curiosity about the world around them; the results of such research typically bring about a significant change in the participants' perspective on, beliefs about, and/or ability to manipulate and interact with their own environment. We might usefully label these most inclusive "grassroots" levels of participation *transformative;* this is the level of participation that Public Laboratory seeks to embody in its approach.

Overview of Public Lab Methodology

Public Lab was formed after the Deepwater Horizon oil spill out of the recognition that 1) the public faces many barriers to accessing key environmental science and health research, and 2) traditional models of citizen science seem inadequate to overcome these barriers. From a practical standpoint, most commonly used monitoring methods involve tools which are far too expensive for the typical citizen to purchase or build themselves, restricting the practice of data collection to those experts and institutions which can afford to purchase such equipment. There also exist more systemic, cultural barriers to the public's participation in science: In the most common modes of citizen science (the *instrumental* mode, discussed above), researchers enlist the public by asking them to contribute data points about a phenomenon local to them (e.g., acquire data via a smart phone "app," or enter information into an online form); this data is then usually collected centrally, curated, and analyzed by experts; the methods and outcomes of the resultant analysis are seldom presented to the citizen participants. This common dynamic in citizen science creates a knowledge gap between the "expert" researcher and the person collecting data "on the ground," and discourages those citizens involved from feeling that they are co-owners of the research process—in fact, it structurally denies them full partnership in the research. Public Lab is interested in bridging this knowledge gap, and in finding avenues for the public to engage in a more *transformative* mode of scientific research in which they share equal ownership of all elements of the research they undertake.

One of the ways that Public Lab has tried to accomplish such a transformation is to employ a "civic technoscience" approach to environmental monitoring. The research tools that Public Lab creates are *open source*, which means that these tools can be modified and spread in a manner that enables them to take on new, unanticipated features and applications as research instruments, and allows for ready dissemination and scaling among and within user communities. Public Lab's use of open source licenses for its collaboratively designed tools, as well as the direct and constant involvement of the community in identifying applications for and developing and employing these tools, also ensures that a) the hardware and software that results from this process is not exclusively owned by any single actor, and, just as importantly, that b) the data collected with these tools is owned by those who collected it. This is a methodology that embraces and supports the public as "experts within their own environment." Encouragingly, Public Lab's application of this methodology has begun to result in a demonstrable shift in the manner in which researchers interact with citizen-generated science—researchers view themselves as contributing to projects that are owned by an entire community, of which they are a part.

To create a workflow that addresses the above-identified barriers to public access to environmental science research and monitoring, we propose that Public Lab has followed these "nine points of engagement" when developing its tools:

- **Engage researchers, not subjects.** The Public Lab process values those working on projects as researchers, not as participants or subjects to be studied.
- **Pull complexity off the shelf.** Simple hacks to off-the-shelf consumer technologies co-opt industry research budgets, hijacking familiar consumer experiences and converting them into sophisticated data collection devices—as well as re-imagining our relationship to the manufactured environment.
- **Build in openness and accountability**. Civic science is social. In the example of aerial maping, anyone can follow the kite string back to the people on the ground, who, in contrast to observation by drone, plane, or satellite, have to explain who they are and why they are there—to make face-to-face contact. The data is linked to an on-the-ground experience which is in turn tied to the community.
- **Create collaborative workflows**. Public Lab creates web platforms on publiclab.org that involve and engage people in every stage of data processing. These collaborative, open source systems enable people with different types of expertise to engage, create and work together.
- **Maintain public data archives**. Public Lab hosts a public archive to legitimize local data through clean, easy presentation and instant access to the technical languages of power—in the instance of aerial mapping, allowing anyone to export data into whichever industry-standard format they require.
- **Mainstream true accountability**. Public Lab's mapping archives sync with Google Earth historical data, and are often republished in Google Maps' base layer, entering the contemporary archive of record for satellite imagery; this lends Public Lab's maps mainstream legitimacy, and provokes a direct confrontation with existing technologies of power.
- **Let images communicate complexity**. Photographic images are more approachable and accessible than re-projected tabular or even graphed data. Public Lab tools produce quantitative data sets that can be expressed in technological languages of power, but we prefer visual data that is contextualized and legible.
- **Protect openness with viral licensing**. The open licenses that the Public Lab community uses guarantee that users of Public Lab tools will be free to use, adapt, reproduce, and redistribute the designs forever—nobody has exclusive control over the intellectual property. For contributors, it helps to create a collaborative network where your work must be attributed and everyone must share improvements under the same terms.
- **Local modification**. Open source licenses allow for tool modifications and adapttions to spread and scale in an "infectious" manner—passing between community members freely in a peer-to-peer manner. They scale not just in terms of growth, but also horizontally as they are adapted to numerous localized grassroots monitoring needs.

To highlight a specific example of Public Lab's methodology in action, the final section of this chapter details Public Lab's recent work in the Gowanus Canal.

Case Study: Gowanus Canal

New York City's Gowanus Canal has recently become a hotbed of ecological design, with a high concentration of non-profit organizations, creative studios, and residents taking direct action in this high profile, but low-lying area of Brooklyn's industrial/post-industrial waterfront. Within this particularly high-capacity context, local community members have been applying Public Laboratory's tools and methodology in their environmental research and advocacy, demonstrating the sort of transformative citizen participation in science that Public Lab aims to facilitate.

The Gowanus Canal came into existence in the late 1800s through landfilling, dredging, and bulkheading a tidal estuary to facilitate industry, shipping, transportation, drainage, and waste management uses. As of 2010, the US EPA has designated it as a Superfund site, bringing national attention and resources to the contamination. From the EPA Region 2 website: *"Contaminants include PCBs, coal tar wastes, heavy metals and volatile organics. PAH concentrations were found to be as high as 45,000 milligrams per kilogram (4.5%) and the contamination was found to traverse the entire length of the canal. Many of the detected contaminants are known carcinogens."* The canal is crisscrossed with bridges and surrounded with residential neighborhoods where the more pioneering settlers live alongside active industrial sites.

Gowanus Low Altitude Mapping (GLAM) is a local alliance housed at the Gowanus Canal Conservancy, and receives institutional support from local art center Proteus Gowanus and canoe club Gowanus Dredgers. Many professional landscape architects, urban planners, and geographers who live in the area are contributing their professional expertise, time and hardware to GLAM. From its wintry origins in January 2011 where members hand-taped Mylar balloons in the freezing cold, to near weekly kite mapping events in the summer of 2012, GLAM has become a part of the local neighborhood's rhythm and identity. The bright yellow kites and red balloons favored by Public Lab members often attract local children, who arrive on site, bringing their parents along behind them to observe the balloon mapping process. In these ways—through conversations on public sidewalks, and through collaborative and open-source research methods—the advances in understanding yielded by GLAM's process are effectively propagated among researchers and local residents who are directly invested in their own, impacted environment. With these civic science tools, engaging methods, and presentations of data that are visually appealing, or even poetic, a broader sample of the affected community is attracted than would have been by a more traditional science and technology approach. The best of the collected aerial images are then annotated and emailed to the GLAM community (designers/artists/environmental scientists), as well as to local representatives and community boards and the Public Lab community.

More holistically, GLAM seeks to understand the "cyborg body" of the Gowanus Canal—its highly engineered systems which include sewage pumping stations, submerged aeration pipes, active industrial bulkhead for barging, naturalized deteriorating bulkhead, sunken ships, shifting shoals, dredged sediment, and underground chemical plumes left behind from the conversion of coal to natural gas at 3 former manufactured gas plants (MGPs). In order to visualize the number of pipes and outfalls connected to the Gowanus Canal, one might imagine it as a kind of vast, wooly caterpillar, with pipes emerging from all sides like spines. Few of these pipes are properly permitted; many have unknown origins dating back more than a century; some carry the underground contamination the EPA intends to remediate; others flow with sewage even in dry weather. During rain events, the Gowanus Canal receives

Mylar survival blanket balloon operated by the Public Lab and the Gowanus Canal Conservancy capturing aerials of new restoration planting and lost historic springs along Brooklyn's Gowanus Canal Conservancy. Photo: Joshua Weinstein, http://weinsteinfilm.com

more than 370 million gallons of combined sewage and storm water each year (NYC DEP, 2008). GLAM also investigates the waters of the Gowanus, as they are being continually influenced by ocean tides, sewage overflow, pumped-in water from the East River, surface runoff from the surrounding industrial lots, and even freshwater entering via hidden pipes or springs. Further, GLAM has focused on the vegetation found along the Gowanus Canal: spots where particular species thrive by virtue of their elevation above the water; the success of naturalized or self-seeded plants; the progress of the Gowanus Canal Conservancy's own remediatory gardening work; the discovery of new areas for planting; the mapping of urban forest canopy throughout the Gowanus Canal watershed. In addition, some balloon mappers have developed insights into site hydrology by extrapolating from the presence of particular plants that can be associated with drainage patterns: The cracks in the pavement next to an abandoned MTA trolley power station, for example, may indicate the presence of an underground stream.

The questions driving this community investigation closely parallel questions that the EPA is seeking to answer through its Superfund remediation, and Public Lab's situated methodology has provided support for the Superfund process via GLAM's development of new questions, new data sets, and new interpretations of data about the canal. GLAM's data collection and interpretative power are perhaps best demonstrated by the discovery of a freshwater stream and two undocumented pipes entering the Gowanus—discoveries that resulted from Conservancy members' intimate knowledge of the canal, garnered through repeated canoe trips and through grassroots mapping of aerial imagery. In this process, the on-the-ground knowledge of long-term residents helped to highlight small details in the aerial images. The waterways in question were not included in a prior survey conducted by professional hydrologists at CH2M HILL on behalf of the EPA; now, the EPA has integrated the waterways identified by the GLAM community into their cleanup map. Other examples of GLAM contributions include the identification of a multinational company whose circuit boards were found in the canal (Amperex, now owned by Philips), whose circuit boards labeled "Ferroxcube" were identified by Eymund Diegel as part of a truck load of e-waste dumped into the Canal in the 1950s (the company may now be required to make payments into the Superfund). Additionally, poorly insulated buildings burning the highly-polluting heating oil #6, identified in the course of winter imaging; local species survival information that is now assisting the landscape architects overseeing remediation plantings; and the monitoring of plumes from active industries are also GLAM contributions.

GLAM's ability to frame questions about the canal is strengthened because its researchers live in the neighborhoods surrounding the canal and share social bonds and interests; these new questions are pointing towards new means of restoration, exemplified by recent speculation as to the location of the yet-unconfirmed Marylander graveyard, the United States' first veterans' cemetery. The Gowanus Conservancy's Eymund Diegel (also a Public Lab board member) noticed unusual concrete crack patterns in a nearby parking lot; through Diegel's interest in archeology, and his outreach efforts to the New York Historical Society, the cracks are speculated to be the site of the Revolutionary War-era graveyard. Diegel is seeking to build a coalition around restoring the graveyard as a memorial park, and, in the process, funding the creation of a storm water abatement garden near the canal.

GLAM's achievements include having been featured by the *New York Times* in regard to the topics of investigation they have proposed at the Canal. This bolsters Public Laboratory's founding assertion: that environmental investigation is a form of civic media. With aerial pollution spotting now regularly resulting in alerts issued from citizens to the very government agencies that are tasked with regulating the environment, the status quo of top-down environmental management is being inverted. Further evidence of this inversion: GLAM mappers were contacted by the EPA in the immediate aftermath of Hurricane Sandy, and asked to report back on water conditions at the Canal. GLAM and EPA Region 2 are breaking new ground in citizen-government collaboration. GLAM members sit on Superfund community advisory committees, and take questions that arise in Superfund Working Groups out into the field as part of their civic science research efforts, with the result that more data is available for empowered decision-making. Having the immediacy of a snapshot and the geographic accuracy of a satellite, custom aerial imagery builds a communication bridge recognizable to both the community experiencing their environment on a daily basis as well as to governing bodies used to traditional forms of geodata. GLAM is providing new data to Google Earth, to the government, and to public media sources, and this data helps both to shape the official record, and to facilitate the local community's re-engagement with its watershed. Ultimately, this is GLAM's goal—leveraging local expertise in order to generate actionable data for advocacy, action, and a heightened understanding of the environment.

References

Bonney, Rick; Cooper, Caren B. et al. (2009). "Citizen Science: A Developing Tool for Expanding Science Knowledge and Scientific Literacy." *BioScience* 59 (11), pp. 977–984.

Clark, Fiona and Illman, Deborah L. (2001). "Dimensions of Civic Science: Introductory Essay." *Science Communication* 23 (1), pp. 5–27. doi:10.1177/1075547001023001002.

Cohn, Jeffrey P. (2008). "Citizen Science: Can Volunteers Do Real Research?" *BioScience* 58 (3), p. 192. doi:10.1641/B580303.

Cooper, Caren B; Dickinson, Janis; Phillips, Tina and Bonney, Rick (2007). "Citizen Science as a Tool for Conservation in Residential Ecosystems." *Ecology and Society* 12 (2), p. 11.

Crowdsourcing.org, "NASA Launches New Citizen Science Game 'CLOUDS'," http://bit.ly/TUkUjc.

Dickinson, Janis L; Shirk, Jennifer et al. (2012). "The Current State of Citizen Science as a Tool for Ecological Research and Public Engagement." *Frontiers in Ecology and the Environment* 10 (6), pp. 291–297. doi:10.1890/110236.

Dosemagen, Shannon; Warren, Jeff and Wylie, Sara (2011). "Grassroots Mapping: Creating a participatory map-making process centered on discourse." *Journal of Aesthetics and Protest* 8 (Winter 2011/2012), pp. 217–228.

Fortun, Kim and Fortun, Mike (2005). "Scientific Imaginaries and Ethical Plateaus in Contemporary US Toxicology." *American Anthropologist* 107 (1), pp. 43–54.

Fuentes Batista, Martha (2012). "Mapping 'Diversity of Participation' in Networked Media Environments. In review. Available at SSRN: http://ssrn.com/abstract=2191276 or http://dx.doi.org/10.2139/ssrn.2191276.

Goodchild, Michael F. (2007). "Citizens as Sensors: The World of Volunteered Geography." *GeoJournal* 69 (4), pp. 211–221. doi:10.1007/s10708-007-9111-y.

Haklay, Muki (2012). "Citizen Science and Volunteered Geographic Information: Overview and Typology of Participation." In *Crowdsourcing Geographic Knowledge: Volunteered Geographic Information (VGI) in Theory and Practice*, eds. Daniel Z. Sui, Sarah Elwood, and Michael F. Goodchild, pp. 105–122. Berlin: Springer. doi:10.1007/978-94-007-4587-2_7.

Ioannidis, John P. A. (2005). "Why Most Published Research Findings Are False." *PLoS Med* 2 (8): e124. doi:10.1371/journal.pmed.0020124

New York City Department of Environmental Protection, Waterbody/Watershed Facility Plan (2008). Gowanus Canal, P. ES-5.

Silvertown, Jonathan (2009). "A New Dawn for Citizen Science." *Trends in Ecology & Evolution* 24 (9) (September), pp. 467–471. doi:10.1016/j.tree.2009.03.017.

Bejing Air Tracks: Tracking Data for Good

Sarah Williams

One of the biggest barriers to sustainable development in many rapidly developing countries is the lack of data which would allow us to make informed decisions about the places we live. If data exists, it is rarely obtainable or used by those who are charged with development decisions and it often does not land in the hands of the citizens themselves. The ubiquitous nature of mobile devices world-wide has made us all data collectors. While there is much concern about how this data is used by governments and private corporations, and there should be, these ubiquitous data recorders can just as easily be leveraged by citizens for a public good.

An example of this public good can be seen in a project my research lab developed with the Associated Press (AP) to create mobile air quality sensors during the 2008 Beijing Olympics. *Beijing Air Tracks*, as the project was known by the AP, started with a simple question: "Can the Olympics be a way to expose air quality issues in China?" By using our sensors, the Associated Press, not the Chinese Government, became the only organization to report on particulate matter, the fine dust pollutants in the air that could have had the largest effects on athletes during the Olympics. The Chinese government did release what it called an "air quality index;" however, the index was un-interpretable because little information was provided on how the numbers were developed.[1] The Associated Press sensors provided the only real-time, geo-registered measurements for particulate matter and carbon monoxide, and did so at the events the reporters were covering. *Beijing Air Tracks* showed how new technologies could be used to advocate for environmental change and illustrated how anyone can take control of data and inform the public at large. The lessons learned from this experiment go beyond exposing air quality conditions in China, as the devices developed showed that ubiquitous computing, such as mobile phones, can allow us to take control of information and use it to advocate for change.

When the project was conceived in 2007, there was much conversation in the press about whether the Beijing City Government would be able to clean up its act for the Olympics. The *Washington Post*'s Maureen Fan reported that many visitors to Beijing were struck by the grey skies and wondered "how this city can possibly be ready to host them in less than 10 months" (Fan, 2007). London's *Guardian* questioned how Beijing would be able to improve air quality after "more than a million cars were taken off the roads for the four-day test period, but there was no improvement in the air quality" (Watts, 2007). The *New York Times* perhaps summed up the situation best when Jim Yardley said: "Beijing is like an athlete trying to get into shape by walking on a treadmill yet eating double cheeseburgers at the same time" (Yardley, 2007). Factories in and around Beijing were polluting more than ever, while the country claimed to be making a reduction. The reports coming in from Beijing made the task to improve air quality seem impossible.

The Chinese government assured the international community that air quality would be significantly improved by the time of the Olympics. In order to do so, they would put certain policies in place. There were to be widespread shutdowns of factories. Just months before the Olympics, the Chinese government ordered business to suspend operations in Tangshan, one of China's busiest steel centers, about 90 miles from Beijing. The Chinese government also wanted to address air quality on the congested roadways and removed over 3.3 million cars from the streets by mandating alternative day traffic regulations for vehicles with even and odd license plate numbers. The *Washington Post* reported that as the Olympics approached, an additional 220 factory closures were made in Tianjin City and Hebei province, as air quality did not seem to be improving just days before the Olympics. Beijing also extended measures

A montage of photos taken of Associated Press reporters while they were measuring particulate matter and carbon monoxide during the Olympics in Beijing 2008. Photos credited to Sarah Williams and Cressica Brazier

to include a ban on construction during the Olympics (Fan, 2008). Many eyes, including the International Olympic Committee, were anxious to see if Beijing's policies would decrease their problematic air pollution during the Olympics.

Governmental regulatory agencies, including the EPA and the World Health Organization, are largely concerned with chemicals found in the air that contribute to smog. Smog is comprised of particulate matter (PM10), ground level ozone, nitrogen oxide, sulfur dioxide, and carbon monoxide.[2] Fine particulate matter is a broad name given to particles of liquids and solids that pollute the air. PM 10 can be breathed deeply into your lungs and will stay there, causing health problems. Fine particles, defined as PM 10, can stay in the air longer and travel farther than larger particles sizes (WHO, 2006). It should be noted that the United States uses a smaller fine particulate size, PM2.5, as its standard, creating stricter regulations for reductions of these pollutants that can cause adverse health conditions. Ground-level ozone (O3) is not emitted directly into the air, but forms when nitrogen oxide and volatile organic compounds (VOCs) from vehicle exhaust, factory emissions and other sources react with sunlight. It is called the "bad ozone" because if you breathe it in, it can cause various health problems. Nitrogen oxide (NO) is a reddish-brown gas that smells foul; it contributes to acid rain and has adverse effects on water quality. Sulfur dioxide (SO2) combines with volatile organic compounds (VOCs) and sunlight, creating ground-level ozone (WHO, 2006). According to the US Environmental Protection Agency, "carbon monoxide is an odorless, tasteless, colorless gas. At high levels, it can be life threatening."[3] In urban areas, carbon monoxide is a temporary atmospheric pollutant largely resulting from vehicular traffic. In developing countries, carbon monoxide pollution in urban areas can also come from coal-burning stoves that might be used for roadside cooking. Carbon monoxide is often measured along with particulate matter to understand urban air quality microclimates, because carbon monoxide does not travel far and usually expresses highly localized conditions (Kaur et al., 2007; Flachsbart, 1999).

The local air pollution sensors needed to be highly mobile and portable, so we had to limit the amount of pollutants we could measure. We chose to measure pollutants that would tell us the most about the environmental conditions that would impact the athletes, while also testing Chinese government policies that were meant to improve those conditions. We focused on collecting fine particulate matter and carbon monoxide measurements. Fine particulate matter was critical for telling the story of air quality in Beijing, as it is the pollutant that would have the largest effect on athlete performance and related most directly to the Chinese mandate to have widespread factory shutdowns (Harrison and Yin, 2000). Largely powered by coal, Chinese factories are arguably the largest contributors to particulate matter pollution (Hao and Wang, 2005). The regional factory shutdowns were mandated because particulate matter can travel long distances in the air and the Chinese government was unsure how the regional pollution would affect Beijing. It should be noted that particulate matter can be detected in MODIS satellite data and, therefore, the interpretation of MODIS images can provide general measurements of the regional levels of this air pollutant. While this data was helpful for gauging regional air quality levels, it was not used for this study because air quality conditions can be highly localized, and we wanted to know the on-the-ground conditions the athletes were experiencing. While there are several pollutants associated with traffic conditions, we chose carbon monoxide, as we felt that it was the pollutant most understandable to the public. Real-time carbon monoxide sensors have been available longer than many air pollutants. As a result, the sensors had been developed to be more compact and a bit more cost-effective.

The fast-paced news of the Olympics meant we needed air quality sensors that could measure data in real-time. Real-time sensors have different levels of accuracy when compared with static sensors, which are usually left on rooftops and designed to better handle sensing anomalies caused by wind and climate conditions. The team realized our mobile sensors might have some differences in measurement levels from other static devices. However, we believed that exposing the conditions with a full disclosure of possible errors was better than not exposing the air quality conditions at all. The team also knew that we might find pollution levels to be so high that if we under-counted the data, the recordings would still show air levels dangerously above World Health Organization standards.[4] More importantly, the air quality sensors were not compared against the measurements of the statics sensors, but to each other, which created similar accuracy levels. When using any measurement device, accuracy levels will come into question, but given that the team was trying to get a rough estimate of what was happening in real time, and that we fully disclosed the possible errors, we knew the sensors we used were the best fit to allow us to tell the story of air pollution in Beijing.

Real-time particulate matter sensors use optical technology, which measure the shadows of the fine particles as air passes through a light component. We purchased an optical sensor developed by MICRODUST which, at the time of the 2008 Olympics, was considered one of the best optical sensors in the field. There is some discussion in the scientific community about the accuracy of optical sensors versus mass-based sensors, with arguments for both. We believe that, when calibrated, these real-time sensors are the only way to obtain the best estimate of the amount of particulate matter in Beijing's air (Baltrenas and Kvasauskas, 2005; Giugliano et al, 2005).[5] Mass-based devices pump air into filter bags; once the particles are trapped, the bags they are sent to a lab, where they can be measured and analyzed for composition and size.[6] While there are benefits to using filter bags, including a particle composition analysis, they would not have provided real-time reporting.

The carbon monoxide sensor measured CO levels using chemical reactions. Chemical-based sensors have decreased levels of accuracy the longer they are used, because the chemical agent in the sensor degrades. We purchased new carbon monoxide sensors and calibrated these sensors before leaving for Beijing. The particulate matter sensors were much more expensive than the carbon monoxide sensors, because the optical technology needed for these types of sensors is more complex than the chemical detectors for carbon monoxide. It should be noted that just in the last year there have been developments in optical sensors which have made them smaller and cheaper (Mead, 2013).[7] Both devices were connected to GPS receivers and the sensor data was given a geographic location based on the time records associated with the GPS and sensor data points. Once each sensor measurement was given a latitude and longitude, the data was sent back to the main press center via phone.

Weeks before the Olympics started we gave the sensor devices to several reporters and set out to collect recordings in diverse but well-known locations throughout Beijing. The team focused on performing daily recordings in the Olympic Park, Tiananmen Square, and the Temple of Heaven. Just days before the beginning of the Olympics, our ambitious data plans had to change. Several of the Associated Press photographers, who had been given the devices, were questioned by the Chinese government for photographs they had taken. Surveillance of the reporters was cause for concern, and the Associated Press took many reporters off the project because they were worried the Chinese government might detain them. The Associated Press therefore limited the data sensing team to a few reporters. The team focused their work in two areas: 1) Developing a data visualization showing the particulate matter levels in the Olympic Park; 2) Measuring carbon monoxide on the marathon routes before and after the removal of half the cars on the roadways.

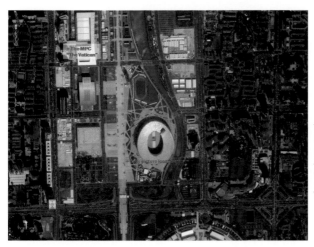

This image shows the location of daily air quality measurements taken by Associated Press reporters on the Olympic Green. Images created by Sarah Williams

The Olympic Park data visualization focused on presenting particulate matter data recordings that were contextualized by international standards and compared to air quality levels in New York and London during the same time. The visualization also used photographs to capture the atmospheric conditions, which often looked like a hazy soup on poor air quality days. It should be noted that the Beijing government officially referred to good air quality levels as "Blue Sky Days" (Fan, 2007). "Blue Skies" could be seen in many of the Bird's Nest pictures. The data for the interactive graphic was collected by an Associated Press reporter who walked the Olympic Green the same time every day. He took a picture of the Bird's Nest from the same vantage point, while also collecting air quality data through the sensor. Pictures of the Bird's Nest Stadium on every day during the Olympics were used to navigate the interactive data visualizations which showed the average mid-afternoon air quality around the Olympic Green, and compared those numbers with average readings in London and New York for the same day. The data visualization revealed that the air quality in Beijing was often at a level 10–20 times higher than what was seen in New York City, and often did not meet the World Health Organization standards (World Health Organization, 2006). New data was added to the visualization daily and Associated Press member newspapers picked up the visualization and posted it on their various web sites.

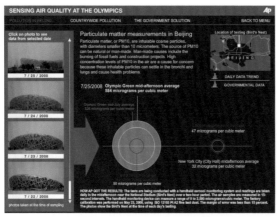

Interactive graphic of particulate matter on the Olympic Green made available to Associated Press member institutions. Image created by Sarah Williams and Siemond Chan from the Associated Press, 2008

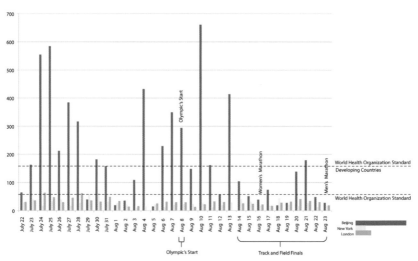

Graph of raw data for the particulate matter sensor used on the Olympic Green by the Associated Press during the Olympics. The graph shows Beijing in comparison to New York and London for the same days. Beijing has levels often 10 times higher than New York City and way above the World Health Organization standards. Image by Sarah Williams

The interactive graphic was just as important for communicating the air quality experience in Beijing as the raw data collected by the sensors. Data measurement reports from the Associated Press about the air quality were picked up by Associated Press subscribers and incorporated in stories across the globe. Observations of the particulate matter results show that air quality was over the World Health Organization standards for much of the Beijing Olympics, except for the last week when it rained. Rain molecules latch onto the fine particles, bringing them to the ground and clearing the sky. The Chinese government was certainly lucky to have rain during the track and field events, where particulate matter would have had the most effect on the participants.

The visualization of the Olympic Green was complimented by a data visualization that took advantage of the highly mobile nature of the sensors. This info graphic showed geo-registered air quality measurements taken along the Olympic marathon route before and after the Chinese government ordered 3.3 million cars removed from the roadway. Developed in coordination with the *New York Times*, the info graphic focused on carbon monoxide levels because they were more closely associated with vehicle exhaust. We compared the figures in Beijing to measurements obtained on New York City's Marathon route for the same day. An analysis of the data conveyed through the visualizations showed that in many areas along the Olympic route, air quality was reduced by almost half, and levels overall were comparable to what would be found in New York City on the same days. The marathon route was a great way to tell the story of air quality. It was an event readers could connect with and contextualize. It should be noted that particulate matter measurements along the route were also captured, but remained fairly close to the numbers at the Olympic Green. The marathon route became a more compelling story using the CO measurements, which showed that car traffic restrictions did help CO emission in some parts of Beijing.

Overall, air quality conditions during much of the Olympics were at a level higher than World Health Organization standards. Exposing the air quality allowed the press to discuss the topic with real numbers, while the government was largely talking about the poor air quality conditions simply as fog, not smog. Having the measurements allowed us to discuss this statement in more specific terms and provide a fact-based counter opinion to the smog argument. The government's air quality index, which ranged from 1–500, was hard to interpret and Beijing government had to essentially tell reporters what the index meant (Fan, 2008). Often the government simply interpreted the results as "Blue Sky Days," meaning the air quality was good, not bad. Having real measurements during the Olympics allowed a real conversation to happen in the press about air quality conditions for the athletes and, more largely, for Beijing residents who would be affected by the air quality after the Olympics were over. Yet measuring the data alone did not change the conversation. By creating compelling graphics for a large, captivated Olympic audience, we were able to bring the story of air quality in Beijing to people all over the world.

Fast-paced development seen in many of the BRIC (Brazil, Russia, India, China) countries, and especially in China, is often associated with high costs to the environment. In China, one of the biggest concerns over the last 10-15 years has been the deterioration of the air quality. Yet with much environmental sensing equipment being controlled by the government and released as indexes, it has been almost impossible to know the true level of air pollution that exists in China, among other countries. Using new, portable environmental sensing devices like the ones developed for the

OLYMPICS
BEIJING '08

'I just ran the first 50 meters, then I looked around
to make sure I was safe and I shut it off.'
USAIN BOLT of Jamaica, who coasted through early-round qualifying in the 100 meters

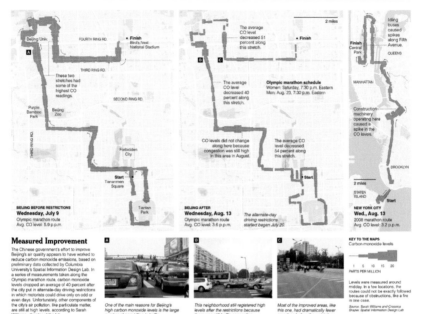

Carbon monoxide measurements along the Olympic marathon route, before and after the Beijing City Government restricted 3.3 million cars from the roadways during the Olympics. The results shows air quality conditions similar to what would be seen along New York City's marathon route. Image by Archie Tse and Sarah Williams

Beijing Olympics allows anyone to test and release air quality measurements in areas where no other data exists. Armed with information, citizens everywhere are empowered to start a conversation with their government about air quality conditions. These types of citizen sensing projects rarely occur in places such as China, where government control of data is tight, and air quality conditions are at levels way above what is recommended by the World Health Organization. We hope our model for data collection shows how the power of mobile phones and new sensor technology can be harnessed to tell a story about the places where we live, giving citizens the possibility to change the places where they live.

References

Baltrenas, Pranas and Kvasauskas, Mindaugas (2005). "Experimental Investigation of Particle Concentration Using Mass and Optical Methods." *Journal of Environmental Engineering and Landscape Management*, XIII(2), pp. 57–64.

Fan, Maureen (2007). "Gray Wall Dims Hopes of 'Green' Games; China Has Vowed to Curb Pollution Before '08 Olympics, but Its Secrecy Is Feeding Skepticism." *Washington Post*, 16 October 2007, p. A01.

Fan, Maureen (2008). "If That Doesn't Clear the Air …; China, Struggling to Control Smog, Announces 'Just-in-Case' Plan." *Washington Post,* 31 July 2008, p. A01.

Flachsbart, Peter G. (1999). "Human exposure to carbon monoxide from mobile sources." *Chemosphere: Global Change Science*, 1, pp. 301–329.

Giugliano, Michele, et al. (2005). "Particulate (PM2.5–PM1) at urban sites with different traffic exposure." *Atmospheric Environment*, 39, pp. 2421–2431.

Hao, Jiming and Wang, Litao (2005). "Improving Urban Air Quality in China: Beijing Case Study." *Air & Waste Manage. Assoc.*, 55, pp. 1298–1305.

Harrison, Roy M. and Yin, Jianxin (2000). "Particulate matter in the atmosphere: which particle properties are important for its effects on health?" *Science of the Total Environment*, 249 (1), pp. 85–101.

Kaur, Soni, Nieuwenhuijsen, Mark J. and Colvile, Roy N. (2007). "Fine particulate matter and carbon monoxide exposure concentrations in urban street transport microenvironments." *Atmospheric Environment*, 41, pp. 4781–4810.

Mead, M. I., et al. (2013). "The use of electrochemical sensors for monitoring urban air quality in low-cost, high-density networks." *Atmospheric Environment*, 70, pp. 186–203.

Paulos, Eric, Honicky, R.J. and Hooker, Ben (2009). "Citizen Science: Enabling Participatory Urbanism." *Handbook of Research on Urban Informatics: The Practice and Promise of the Real-Time City*. Ed. Marcus Foth. Hershey, PA: Information Science Reference, IGI Global.

Street, David G., et al. (2007). "Air Quality during the 2008 Beijing Olympic Games." *Atmospheric Environment*, 41, pp. 480–492.

Watts, Jonathan (2007). "China prays for Olympic wind as car bans fail to shift Beijing smog." *The Guardian*, 21 Aug. 2007.

World Health Organization (2006). WHO Air Quality Guidelines for particulate matter, ozone, nitrogen dioxide and sulfur dioxide; Global update 2005, Summary of Risk. Geneva: World Health Organization.

Yardley, Jim (2007). "Beijing's Olympic Quest: Turn Smoggy Sky Blue." *New York Times*, 29 Dec. 2007.

Yardley, Jim (2008). "In Beijing, Blue Skies Prove Hard to Achieve." *New York Times*, 28 July 2008.

Zhang, Wei; Guo, JingHua; Sun, YeLe; Yuan, Hui; Zhuang, GuoShun; Zhuang, YaHui and Hao, ZhengPing. (2007). "Source apportionment for urban PM10 and PM2.5 in the Beijing area." *Chinese Science Bulletin*, (52) 5, March 2007, pp. 608–615.

---

1 And, therefore, the numbers were only interpretable by the Chinese government themselves.

2 The 2005 *WHO Air quality guidelines* (AQGs) set acceptable levels of these various substances in the air for countries worldwide.

3 Cf. http://www.epa.gov/iaq/co.html.

4 The sensors were calibrated for air quality conditions in Beijing.

5 Baltrenas and Kvasauskas (2005) tested optical and mass particulate matter sensing tools and found the optical sensors were usually above the mass sensors. This goes against previous claims that mass-based particulate matter sensors are usually better quality.

6 One benefit of using mass devices is that the analysis of bag contents provides information about the types of particles which can help determine the likely source of the pollutants.

7 According to the Seeed Wiki (http://www.seeedstudio.com/wiki/Grove_-_Dust_Sensor), the Grove Dust Sensor "measures the particulate matter level in air by counting the Lo Pulse Occupancy time (LPO time) in given time unit. LPO time is in proportion to PM concentration. This sensor can provide you pretty reliable data for your PM2.5 project or air purifier system because it's still responsive to particulates whose diameter is 1μm." It is roughly a little bigger than a quarter.

Legibility from Below

Dietmar Offenhuber

In *Seeing Like a State*, James C. Scott describes a fundamental problem of governance: knowing where things are and what people do. In order to make decisions, set policies, collect taxes and allocate budgets, the state has to get a sense of what happens and what is needed on the ground; the state's territory has to be made legible. This has happened through birth registers, cadastral maps, and even through the introduction of family names — all deliberate inventions that everyone takes for granted today. Scott emphasizes that these tools are not only used to describe, but also to prescribe. They impose an order in society and make sure that everything is in a place where it can be found again; states tend to have a problem with people who move around a lot. Legibility is consequently not just a method of abstraction and analysis, but also an instrument of rule and, occasionally, oppression, especially when the imposed standards and representations override and replace local knowledge and conventions. This concept of "legibility from above" is central to a high-modernist ideology, placing the primacy of science, efficiency and rationality — which in some instances have led to well-known catastrophic outcomes involving destructive urban renewal and large-scale social engineering.

However, by only considering an observer from above, Scott's notion of legibility misses an important aspect. There are instances in which local and implicit knowledge is not enough to make sense of a situation; in which people need to establish "legibility from below," a higher-level coordination emerging from the bottom up, in order to address issues that transcend the local realm.

This concerns, first of all, the legibility of the state itself, whose constituents want to know what happens to their tax money, whether today's air quality is worse than ten years ago, or how their trash is disposed of. Rendering itself legible to its constituents and therefore controlling itself is considered a central principle of the democratic state. As the policy scholar Andreas Schedler puts it: "The great difficulty lies in this: You must first enable the government to control the governed; and in the next place oblige it to control itself" (Schedler, 1999, p. 13). Top-down transparency measures in the form of Freedom of Information laws and Open Data policies are designed to prevent corruption by allowing citizens to evaluate government and corporate actions.[1] As US Supreme Court Justice Louis D. Brandeis famously noted at the beginning of the 20th century, "Sunlight is said to be the best of disinfectants; electric light the most efficient policeman" (Brandeis, 1914, p. 92).

However, the concept of total transparency is both too strong and too weak at the same time. It is too strong, because full and absolute transparency is difficult to achieve where humans make decisions, and is probably also not desirable, as it would make it very difficult to make any decisions at all. At the same time, the notion of absolute transparency is too weak, because it implicitly assumes that all relevant information already exists in a central place, and that this information can be regarded as truthful and reliable. Of course, not every piece of information generated by a bureaucracy is useful or relevant for its citizens, but at the same time it is also impossible to anticipate which kind of information might become relevant one day. A deeper problem with Open Data initiatives is that they tend to focus on questions of access, rather than the production of information itself. In other words, instead of enabling a true "legibility from below" that combines local knowledge within a high-level framework, Open Data portals are like a mirror image reflecting the state's perspective from above, often without the context necessary to fully understand this picture.

Accountability Versus Transparency

Accountability goes beyond transparency and questions of information access and exchange. In our context, accountability can be defined as the obligation of power-holders, whether they are public officials, private corporations, financial institutions and other organizations, to take responsibility for their actions (Malena, Forster and Singh, 2004).

Accountability involves answerability—the power-holders have to be ready to answer questions and justify their actions, regardless of what information might already exist. Secondly, accountability also involves enforcement; evidence of abuse and corruption has to be followed by consequences. Both elements, answerability and enforcement, are necessary; answerability without enforcement is ultimately frustrating and pointless (Joshi, 2010, p. 20). Furthermore, accountability does not need or expect full transparency. As Andreas Schedler explains, "Agents of accountability do not pretend to supervise everything. In fact, they assume that nothing close to close oversight is taking place and accept that their genuine field of competence consists of unobserved and often unobservable actions" (Schedler, 1999, p. 20).

While the concept of accountability is old, its approaches have evolved rapidly during the past decade. The traditional means of accountability are state-centered mechanisms such as the separation of powers, administrative oversight structures and, most importantly, elections. Elected officials who got caught misusing their power will not be elected again; companies who violate the rights of their workers will end up in court—so much for the theory. In practice, we know that public accountability instruments have not always been effective. Enforcement might not happen because information required as evidence is not available; elections might fail to address the more nuanced conflicts of interest involved in governance.

In contrast to state-centric accountability mechanisms, social accountability stands for community-driven efforts to establish accountability (Joshi and Houtzager, 2012). Although social accountability is increasingly being initiated and supported by states and development agencies, they often operate from the bottom-up, either taking a formal or an informal route. If the formal route via the legal system is taken, the community has to produce or gain access to relevant information, and make their case in the legal system, often while building alliances with other groups or politicians. All of these activities require a substantial amount of coordination, analysis and often persuasion. If the formal path does not succeed, social accountability initiatives may also choose informal channels—by creating pressure through media campaigns, frequently using "rude" but effective tactics of naming and shaming (Hossain, 2010).

Emerging Practices

History has many examples of social movements that have aimed at demanding accountability via formal and informal means. In most of these examples, the role of the community has mainly focused on communication and creating pressure—making their voices heard and creating impact via demonstrations or advocacy campaigns. Today, we witness the emergence of new, technologically augmented social accountability initiatives that are not limited to the traditional roles of campaigning and community organizing. Their members collectively engage in the systematic collection and analysis of data that withstands scrutiny from experts.

Many recent projects have focused on the collection and dissemination of information. Phenomena such as everyday corruption are notoriously difficult to quantify. "I paid a bribe" is a whistle-blower platform, founded in 2010 by Ramesh and Swati

Ramanathan in Bangalore, that has the goal to document the extent of corruption in Indian society by allowing participants to report instances of corruption they were affected by (Campion, 2011).

Other projects place their emphasis on collaborative data analysis. The GuttenPlag Initiative presented in this volume uncovered evidence on academic plagiarism in the doctoral thesis of the former German defense minister Karl-Theodor zu Guttenberg. The thesis was published and readily available, but to what extent the suspicions of plagiarism were justified was not evidently clear. An online collective painstakingly analyzed every single paragraph of the thesis and identified 135 uncited sources, rendering roughly two-thirds of the text plagiarized, leading to the resignation of the defense minister, a case unprecedented in German history (GuttenPlag Wiki, 2013).

A third group of projects uses the community to work on the political implementation, exemplified by the genesis of Hamburg's recently implemented Transparency Law. After years of fruitless efforts by advocacy groups to make the city implement such a law, a group of citizens decided to write it themselves and submit it to the city senate. Fearing a public backlash and the rise of the transparency-minded German Pirate Party, all ruling parties in the city senate finally supported and implemented the citizen-authored law (Mehr Demokratie e.V., 2012). Citizen-authored legislation is perhaps the most extensive understanding of social accountability.

These three examples highlight aspects that are, to some extent, part of every collaborative accountability initiative—collection, analysis and implementation. Often, initiatives span across multiple communities that are not necessarily driven by the same goal. For example, civic groups in the pre-revolutionary Tunisia of 2010 used photos made by plane spotters—aviation enthusiasts photographing airplanes at different airports in the world—to reconstruct the movement of the Tunisian presidential airplane.

The organizers of a successful project have to navigate and negotiate multiple challenges. The World Bank report on social accountability identifies five "building blocks" for building a successful social accountability campaign. The first step is the mobilization of participants and supporters around an entry point, followed by the collection of an evidence base that withstands scrutiny. The third building block is to go public to raise awareness and support. The fourth step is to build coalitions with journalists, politicians, lawyers and scientists who are instrumental for the final step, negotiating and advocating change (World Bank, 2012). These five central aspects make it clear that such an endeavor is, by its nature, more cooperative than adversarial, with negotiation between different groups and actors with different agendas crucial to the overall success.

The Role of Technology in Social Movements

For a long time, face-to-face interaction was considered essential for building the social relations deemed necessary for running a successful campaign. The potential of the Internet for mobilizing a large number of people has been recognized at least since Jody Williams won the 1997 Nobel Peace Prize for the International Campaign to Ban Landmines, which she organized primarily over the Internet from her home in Putney, Vermont (Putnam, 2001).

In today's popular discourse, the idea that social media and the Internet play a central role in social movements it is all but taken for granted. However, the exact role of technology is still somewhat controversial. One of the most vocal critics of technology-centric thinking, Evgeny Morozov, argues that the Internet by itself does not have

Large inflatable rat, used in labor union demonstrations as an informal accountability instrument for shaming businesses that employ non-union labor. This example was photographed on 46th Road, between 5th Street and Vernon Blvd, in Long Island City, Queens, NY., 12 September 2012. Photo: Roy Smith, https://commons.wikimedia.org/wiki/File:Union-rat.jpg.

an inherent logic or a democratizing effect; such a "naïve belief in the emancipatory nature of online communication that favors the oppressed rather than the oppressor" overstates the role of information and ignores underlying power structures (Morozov, 2012, p. xiii).

However, communication technology intervenes at a more fine-grained level—at the interface between different actors and social groups. The success of Internet campaigning, for example, results from the almost non-existent cost of participation, compared with traditional volunteering, in terms of time and effort. On the one hand, this greatly amplifies the scope and speed of public engagement. On the other hand, such a low threshold of participation, or "slacktivism," has also been seen as responsible for civil disengagement and for what Putnam called a rising "imbalance between talking and listening." As John Seely Brown and Paul Duguid point out, "the ability to send a message to president@whitehouse.gov ... can give the illusion of much more access, participation, and social proximity than is actually available" (Brown and Duguid, 2000; Putnam, 2001).

As other chapters in this volume, especially the interview with Patrick Meier, demonstrate, social capital, the critique of "slacktivism," is largely unfounded; personal commitment and civic engagement are not diminished by digital means of communication; often quite the opposite takes place. The five building blocks of social accountability campaigns offer a useful guide for estimating the specific roles and limitations of social media at a specific stage of the project.

Criticisms of Community-Based Action

Community-based and participatory modes of governance are almost universally accepted as desirable and assumed to automatically lead to a more just and inclusive society. However, it should not be forgotten that community-based action represents the interests of that specific community, which is not necessarily aligned with the greater public good. This can raise a number of concerns:

Mob Mentality: Informal sanctions can quickly lead to mob mentality, bypassing formal processes by choice rather than necessity. This is exasperated by the tendency of transparency mechanisms to make failure more visible than success—creating easy targets for what Larry Lessig calls "gotcha journalism." Some developments in the community of crowd-based plagiarism hunters support these concerns, and show that a legitimate accountability tool can quickly become the domain of bounty hunters hired to damage an individual's reputation.

Vulnerability: Despite their reputation, bottom-up, decentralized initiatives are not as resilient and incorruptible as is often assumed. As Lawrence Lessig points out in his interview in this volume, citizen-authored legislation is especially vulnerable to subversion by special interest groups. In fact, many tactics of digital protesters have already been adopted by state entities and corporations.[2] According to the principles of collective action, a small, but well-coordinated group is in a better position to promote their interests compared to a large, heterogeneous group (Olson, 1965).

Intransparency: Ironically, internet-organized social accountability campaigns often struggle with opacity themselves. Official, centralized data repositories might be subject to all kinds of systematic biases, or may be hampered by incompleteness or inaccessibility. But at least their problems are known, can be scrutinized, and taken into account. Distributed data, on the other hand, generated by an anonymous collective, have many "unknown unknowns." The underlying assumption of the authenticity of public discourse on the Internet is increasingly called into question. Companies and state agencies have started to use what is called "persona management software," platforms for simulating a bottom-up discourse across popular social media sites. Also known by the term "astroturfing," these software platforms deploy a remote-controlled army of fake, digital people who participate in public forums in order to manipulate public opinion. These "personas" have detailed personal backgrounds, to make them seem authentic to outside observers, and engage in a lively discourse with each other to change or displace other discussions (Monbiot, 2011).

Hidden Agendas: Community governance and bottom-up volunteer initiatives have also been used to promote an agenda of deregulation and dismantling of public services. Recently, British Prime Minister David Cameron's signature policy of the "Big Society," embracing community governance and volunteering, has been extensively criticized by those same volunteer organizations for depriving them of much-needed public funding.

Perverse Incentives: Finally, even with the best of intentions and perfect execution, the results of transparency initiatives can result in the opposite of what was intended.

As a transparency measure, Supreme Court Judge Brandeis, mentioned earlier, implemented the mandatory publication of bankers' compensations as a way of shaming bankers into modesty. The measure actually had the opposite effect, becoming an incentive to get more (Lessig, 2009). Similar concerns have been raised for the "I paid a bribe" initiative, by revealing the market price for corruption, actually consolidating instead of preventing it.

Reconciling Activists and Power-Holders

On the surface, social accountability efforts seem adversarial and polarizing. I hope this short essay made it clear that this is not the case. They can only be successful if they are built upon cooperation, alliances—among the participants, but also connected to outside—the media, politicians. Ultimately, they are depending on cooperation with the power-holders they are holding accountable. Governments sometimes still perceive accountability initiatives as a threat, often conflating their efforts with the agenda of the political opposition. However, especially in the international development domain, social accountability has become a central hope for better governance and service delivery. Governments and funding agencies building roads, infrastructure or housing projects need accountability mechanisms to know how effectively their funding is spent, how well their services are implemented. "Governments are all about delivering, but they are on the top and don't see what is happening on the ground," Randson Mwadiwa, Secretary to the Treasury of Malawi, recently said at the World Bank Panel on Social Accountability (World Bank 2012). By including voices that are normally not included, social accountability mechanisms can complement and enhance conventional mechanisms. In this sense, social accountability becomes a tool for mutual legibility, a manifestation of the abstract idea of the social contract between citizens and their representatives.

References

Brandeis, Louis Dembitz (1914). *Other People's Money: And How the Bankers Use It*. New York: F. A. Stokes.

Brown, John Seely and Duguid, Paul (2000). *The Social Life of Information*. Boston: Harvard Business School Press.

Campion, Mukti Jain (2011). "Paid a Bribe? Tell Everyone About It." *BBC*, June 5, sec. South Asia. http://www.bbc.co.uk/news/world-south-asia-13616123.

GuttenPlag Wiki (2013). Accessed March 5. http://de.guttenplag.wikia.com/wiki/GuttenPlag_Wiki.

Hossain, Naomi (2010). "Rude Accountability: Informal Pressures on Frontline Bureaucrats in Bangladesh." *Development and Change* 41 (5), pp. 907–928. doi:10.1111/j.1467-7660.2010.01663.x.

Joshi, Anuradha (2010). "Do They Work? Assessing the Impact of Transparency and Accountability Initiatives in Service Delivery." *Development Policy Review*. http://www.dfid.gov.uk/R4D/PDF/Outputs/Mis_SPC/60827_DPRJoshi_Preprint.pdf.

Joshi, Anuradha and Houtzager, Peter (2012). "Widgets or Watchdogs? Conceptual Explorations in Social Accountability." *Public Management Review* 14 (2), pp. 145–162.

Lessig, Lawrence (2009). "Against Transparency." October 9. http://www.tnr.com/print/article/books-and-arts/against-transparency.

Malena, Carmen, Forster, Reiner and Singh, Janmejay (2004). "Social Accountability - An Introduction to the Concept and Emerging Practice." Social Development Paper No. 76. Washington, DC: The World Bank.

Monbiot, George (2011). "The Need to Protect the Internet from 'Astroturfing' Grows Ever More Urgent." *The Guardian*. http://www.guardian.co.uk/environment/georgemonbiot/2011/feb/23/need-to-protect-internet-from-astroturfing.

Morozov, Evgeny (2012). *The Net Delusion: The Dark Side of Internet Freedom*. New York: PublicAffairs.

Olson, Mancur (1965). *The Logic of Collective Action: Public Goods and the Theory of Groups.* Boston: Harvard University Press.

Putnam, Robert D. (2001). *Bowling Alone: The Collapse and Revival of American Community*. New York: Simon and Schuster.

Schedler, Andreas (1999). "Conceptualizing Accountability." *The Self-Restraining State: Power and Accountability in New Democracies*. Boulder, CO: Lynne Rienner Publishers, pp. 13–28.

World Bank (2012). "Round Table Discussion with Jim Yong Kim on Social Accountability and the Science of Delivery." *World Bank Live Webcast*. December 6. http://live.worldbank.org/round-table-discussion-jim-yong-kim-social-accountability-and-science-delivery-live-webcast.

——— (2012). "Social Accountability Sourcebook Homepage." Accessed October 13. http://www.worldbank.org/socialaccountability_sourcebook/.

1 http://sunlightfoundation.com/blog/2013/02/12/whytransparencymatters

2 http://www.theverge.com/2013/1/28/3924248/ddos-how-a-tool-built-by-web-activists-became-the-ultimate-weapon-for

COMPREHEND

Newspaper Front Page Analysis: How Do They Tell the Story?

Pablo Rey Mazón

1. Introduction

Social Networking Sites (SNS), especially Twitter and Facebook, have played an important role in the current global social movement wave, from the Arab Spring to the Occupy movement in the United States. Social movement actors use SNS, among other tools, to document, promote, support and, in some cases, to coordinate movement activity. SNS have also become key sources of information for observers, both supporters, detractors, and non-participants, as well as for professional journalists working within print, broadcast, and online media, whose reporting strategies have, in some cases, shifted towards curating and incorporating content first circulated via SNS. In the context of increasingly transnationalized media firms and cross-platform convergence, information rapidly flows back and forth between SNS and mass media.

Print newspaper coverage also has an impact far beyond paid subscribers or readers, since it greatly influences broadcast (television and radio) news agendas; newspaper coverage also plays an important agenda-setting role for blogs and social media. The complexity of the converged media ecology requires new approaches to newspaper content analysis, which has long been used by social movement scholars as a proxy for social movement activity. This essay describes an innovative approach to the analysis and visualization of front page newspaper coverage.

2. Background: How Did I Start Coding Front Pages?

On Sunday May 15th, 2011, one week before the municipal elections that were taking place all around the country, there was a grassroots-organized march in many cities in Spain under the motto "Real Democracy Now" (*Democracia Real Ya*[1]). By then, I was living in Boston and closely following all these events through the Internet.

Tens of thousands of people[2] throughout Spain marched on the streets during what later would be known as #15M, the #SpanishRevolution or the 'indignados' movement. The movement was inspired by the Arab Spring and the Icelandic Revolution,[3] and was preceded by previous social mobilizations in Spain. The country was in the midst of a huge economic crisis and suffering from austerity measures that were dismantling the welfare state. The crisis was related to the world economic recession and to the bursting of the real estate bubble. In the short term, this new mobilization was related to #nolesvotes,[4] a mobilization launched and forged on the Internet against Internet censorship that a new law was enforcing. In the years before, there had also been other mobilizations similar to the *Democracia Real Ya* platform involving demonstrations on the streets throughout the country, among others: *Juventud Sin Futuro*,[5] to protest the precarious situation of the youth; *Por una Vivienda Digna*,[6] a citizens' platform created during the real estate bubble crisis to address housing problems.

Democracia Real Ya was a grassroots movement that received no support from any party or union. It was a decentralized organization based on the Internet that opted for a multi-site demonstration, instead of the traditional march in the capital (Madrid). No flags were used nor the "ghosts" of the two Spains from the Civil War; today's two major political parties were also absent. Despite the movement's success, the mainstream media did not pay much attention: It was just another demonstration in an electoral period.

That Sunday night after the march, around 40 people decided to stay in Puerta del Sol (Sánchez, 2011), the central square of Madrid. They wanted to keep on with the mobilization, and managed to convince the police to let them stay in the square during the night. After their first general assembly, they started organizing the first working groups. On the next day, many more people came to show support, and around

300 stayed on to sleep in the square. At 5 a.m. the police evicted them (yokopina, 2011), an act that proved to be the tipping point of the movement. On Tuesday evening, more than 10,000 people crowded into the Puerta del Sol to protest the eviction. By that time, I was absorbed with the #acampadasol hashtag in Twitter, the 24-hour live streaming from soltv.tv, and trying to follow every bit of information about what was happening in my hometown of Madrid.

Some major newspapers were covering the events, but people in social media, mainly Facebook and Twitter, argued that they were not getting enough coverage. On Wednesday, May 18th, the electoral board in Madrid denied the right to march or gather in the square (Junta Electoral Provinical de Madrid, 2011), and that made the protests even more successful than the previous days: Puerta del Sol Square was full again. I tried to visualize the subsequent reactions of the mainstream media to this new event and tweeted my first newspaper front page data visualization (numeroteca, 2011).

On Thursday morning, May 19th, media attention was completely centered on the occupied squares: The protests started filling all the front pages only after the fourth night at Puerta del Sol, after the "tent cities" had already spread all around the country. The front page data visualization became popular after appearing on menéame (menéame, 2011), a Spanish news aggregator site, as it showed the very moment when the protest entered the mass media loop in an easy and comprehensible way. Indeed, it was used by bloggers (Varela, 2011) to reflect on how the media had waited too long to cover the protests. Some journalists also used it to think about how the media should cover these kinds of protests. The following Sunday, one week after the mobilization had started, the elections took place, but the camps and the spirit of change from the 15M movement remained.

The 15M movement was now live on the streets and ready to grow and take infinite shapes and ways of protests. My front page analysis was also making its first steps, and I was ready to start diving into it and testing its possibilities.

How Are Social and Mass Media Related?

Twitter is the tool researchers most frequently use to study information flows that Social Networking Sites enable, because these streams of information are open, allowing anyone to study their data. Facebook is arguably a more important site for spreading news, based on its far higher penetration rate, but as a closed network, the study of the data has not been as easy as with Twitter. We have used front page newspaper coverage analysis to compare newspaper coverage of recent mass protests with social media attention, in particular, in Twitter.

For example, we have compared the use of popular hashtags, the way message "tweets" are tagged in Twitter, in the 15M movement. The most popular hashtags were #acampadasol, #15M, and #spanishrevolution. We have compared the total number of tweets using these hashtags with the front pages of seven major newspapers in Spain. These hashtags had been selected among those most used at the time regarding this movement according to research by the Complex Systems and Networks Group at the University of Zaragoza (BIFI, 2011). The Twitter data came from Trendistic, an online Twitter data visualization provider.

A similar data analysis has been made with the Occupy movement with US newspapers. In this case, the chart (on p. 50) displays both the percentage of surface dedicated to the Occupy movement (red) and the number of tweets from the various related hashtags like: #ows, #occupywallstreet, #occupyLA, #occupyOakland or #occupyBoston.

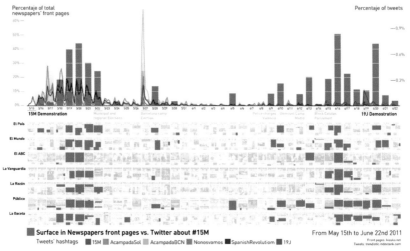

Surface dedicated to the 15M movement in the front page of 7 Spanish newspapers vs. the use of certain Twittter hashtags related to 15M extracted from http://trendistic.indextank.com. From May 15th (left) through June 22nd (right), 2011.

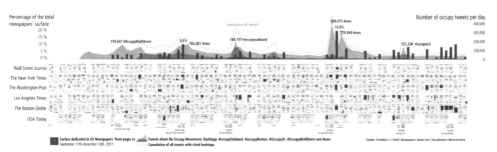

Surface coverage in newspapers front pages vs. Twitter about Occupy from September 17th through December 13th, 2011. The tweets per day come from the data released by r-shief.org in the context of the #occupydatahackathon.

Tweets are instant messages that cover events almost in real time. On the contrary, front pages cover the news of yesterday. Therefore, it is normal to see how different media react to the same event: Twitter coverage peaks the day that it occurs, and press coverage peaks the day after. Following this idea, it is more interesting to explore when Twitter and the press differ: When enormous tweet traffic about an event or action is not followed by that big coverage, or when a week-long, sustained conversation in Twitter around a hashtag doesn't find its way into the print.

3. The Front Page Data Visualization: Building a Tool

The first data visualization started as a "manual" process: I downloaded the images one by one from Kiosko.net, a website providing newspaper front pages from all around the world, and built the array of images with Inkscape, a vector graphics program. Later on, after the good acceptance of the visualization, I started building a script (Rey Mazón, 2011) to allow others to replicate this kind of analysis. Around a year later I started PageOneX, a free software tool (Rey Mazón, 2012a) designed to aid the coding, analysis, and visualization of front page newspaper coverage of major stories and media events.

PageOneX constitutes a straightforward way of interpreting front pages, a very specific piece of the media ecosystem that has direct influence on radio and TV broadcasts. In the past, researchers trying to analyze front pages needed to obtain copies of newspapers, measure column inches by hand (with a physical ruler), and manually input measurements into a spreadsheet or database. This laborious and time-consuming process would be followed by calculation, analysis, and sometimes data visualization. Some of these steps can now be automated, while others can be dramatically simplified.

The process described here is designed to facilitate the relatively rapid creation of "small multiple" data visualizations of front page newspaper coverage. "Small multiple," a term popularized by Edward Tufte, is a kind of data visualization that allows the visual comparison of multiple series of data: Series are displayed separately and placed next to each other. In the case of PageOneX, the displayed data include small images of the newspaper front pages themselves, as well as the surface area on the newspapers' front pages dedicated to a specific news story (a "thread") that runs chronologically along the x-axis (time). Coders manually select the portion of front pages dedicated to that thread. The selected areas are then displayed as shaded or colored transparencies on top of their original front pages. When viewed at sufficiently close range (zoomed in to a story), the text of the original stories that have been coded can still be easily read. However, this form of graphical information display is most compelling on a larger scale: Small thumbnails of the newspaper front pages are arrayed chronologically from left to right, and the viewer is then easily able to see at a glance the evolution of the coverage—or lack of coverage—of a particular news thread over time, as well as to compare different newspapers.

The visual approach allows the reader to have a sense of the coverage and, at the same time, have a look at the very raw data of the analysis, which are the components of the article, whether they be images, headlines or text. These highlighted areas could also be quantified to produce a bar chart. To make the measurements of the areas of news coverage comparable among different newspapers sizes, we use the percentage of used surface, and not the real area in mm².

The basic visualization of this type of graphic displays both the data itself (front pages and highlighted surfaces) as well as the measurement (the percentage of surface area) in a bar or line chart. Bar charts give a more accurate view of the surface devoted to the story, whereas line charts (see below) appear as a more continuous timeline, although they run the risk of suggesting a visual interpolation of discrete data. In other words, newspaper front pages provide one surface area datum per day, so a line connecting two surface area data points (from two consecutive days) produces a false sense of continuity. When different topics are displayed one beside the other, it is a good way to study the battles for attention in the media; how related news "fights" for a position on page one, like in the Arab Spring coverage (Egypt, Syria, Libya and others) in Spanish newspapers (Rey Mazón, 2012b).

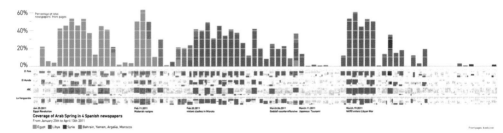

This bar chart shows the percentage of surface coverage used to display news regarding different countries (Egypt, Libya, Syria and others) in the Arab Spring in 4 Spanish newspapers. From January 25th through May 13th 2011. Graphic at: http://www.iecah.org/web/visual/egipto-libia-siria-otros.htm

We can see how the media space is usually focused on one "revolution" at a time, and that there is not much juxtaposition of news about this topic. Moreover, we observed a big drop in the Arab Spring coverage on April 13th, because the Japanese tsunami was breaking news: Note how the green area (Japanese tsunami) "hides" all the other news related to the Arab Spring for a week. It is not the case that "nothing" related to the Arab Spring happened during that week, but rather that the media decided where to pay attention. News on front pages "fights" for space and its areas are related to one another.

Comparing Asynchronous News Coverage in Time

The relative measurement of the surfaces lets us not only compare different news from different newspaper sizes, but also from asynchronous timelines. This method would allow the measurement of the news cycle: enabling us to understand how long news lasts on the front pages and how similar events attract the attention of the media.

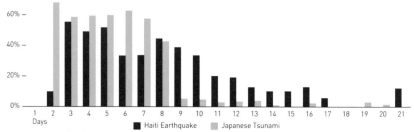

Percentaje of total front page space in 4 Spanish newspapers

In the comparison of the surface coverage dedicated to the Haiti earthquake (Day 1 = January 12th, 2010) and the Japanese tsunami (Day 1 = March 11th, 2011) in four Spanish newspapers, we could measure and compare the length of the coverage. Remarkable is the rapid drop of the Japanese crisis coverage after Day 8 (March 18th, 2011), caused by the UN's authorization allowing the international community to enter the war in Libya.

Semantic Analysis of News Content

It is also possible to make an automatic estimation of the article's content based on semantic technologies. This process would benefit from the automatic transcription of scanned newspaper front pages through optical character recognition (OCR).

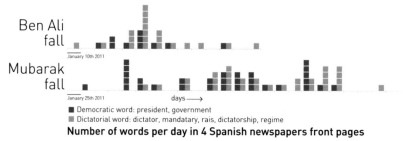

Number of words per day in 4 Spanish newspapers front pages

The fall of Ben Ali (Tunisia, orange) and Hosni Mubarak (Egypt, blue) in 4 Spanish newspapers from January 10th through February 17th, 2011. Source: http://www.iecah.org/web/visual/tunez-egipto.htm

As a case study, we used the fall of Mubarak and Ben Ali to compare how newspapers framed their last government/regime days. We analyzed the number of times that certain words appeared on the front page, and grouped them into two pools:
– Democratic: president, government.
– Dictatorial: dictator, *rais*, dictatorship, regime.
The aim of this study was to measure how newspapers are shifting their vocabulary along time, depending on their support/alignment with the issue they are covering. In Mubarak's fall, we can see how newspapers shifted their frame during the crisis from a predominant use of democratic words (president, government) to more dictatorial ones (dictatorship, dictator, regime). In the case of Ben Ali, more "dictatorial" types of words were employed to describe his last days in power.

Content and Frame Analysis

We have seen how articles can be categorized, then colored and quantified, by multiple taxonomies related to their content: a particular thread or categorized by country. To understand how newspapers are addressing one topic would be not enough to understand how much they are covering it. We will need a framing analysis of their coverage: Are they positive/neutral/negative about it? Are they supportive? How biased is the information they provide?

We used this approach to analyze how different Spanish newspapers were covering corruption cases. The fast-growing list of corruption investigations in Spain (Wikipedia, 2013) contained almost every institution in the country. Everyday, new information and a new case were being unveiled, provoking an increasing sense of indignation. It was also true that the levels of indignation had reached an apex, that they caused either incredulity or insensitivity.

The hypothesis and common knowledge is that every Spanish newspaper is aligned with a political party (Orriols, 2013). Newspapers follow the corruption cases of the "opponent" parties. Measuring front page coverage seemed to be a good proxy to analyze their political agendas and to verify the hypothesis. I selected the most important Spanish newspapers and highlighted the stories related to the different corruption cases during a one-month period.

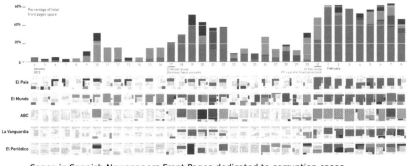

Space in Spanish Newspapers Front Pages dedicated to corruption cases
January 4th - February 8th 2013

By Institution
- PP
- Casa Real
- Varios
- PSOE
- CiU

Frame analysis
- Defensive or positive
- Neutral or negative

Front pages: kiosko.net

Space dedicated to corruption cases in front pages from 5 Spanish newspapers. From January 4th through February 8th 2013. Available at http://pageonex.com/numeroteca/corrupcion-spain-enero-2013

"Guns, Wars and Terrorism." Real size PageOneX
installation at MIT Media Lab, April 2013

In January 2013, the *El Mundo* and *El País* newspapers reported that the ex-treasurer of the ruling party (Partido Popular, PP), Luis Bárcenas, had a $29 million Swiss account (Minder, 2013), and then published excerpts from the party's parallel financial account (*El País*, 2013). Both scoops impelled all the other newspapers to talk about the same PP corruption case, although other corruption cases affecting the main parties were also on the media menu. We coded the corruption cases of the major three parties: PP (conservative), blue; PSOE (center-left social democratic), red; CiU (conservative Catalan nationalist), orange; the royal house, green; other cases, purple.

Both newspapers, *El Mundo* and *El País*, are in opposite political spectrums, but made a common effort in this case to cover the Bárcenas story affecting the conservative party (PP) in the government.

El País centered its coverage on the PP (blue), leaving little space to the CiU (orange) or the monarchy (green), and none to the PSOE (red), following the expected behavior of a party related to the PSOE and the center-left. Meanwhile, *El Mundo* had a colorful timeline illustrating all the major corruption cases. Since the newspaper tends to defend the PP and attack the PSOE, it represented a change in their agenda.

However, some things did not fit into the alignment of mass media with certain major political parties that we could have expected. All of the newspapers were talking about the PP corruption case, but not in the same way. To understand how they were framing the story, we needed to add a new layer to the visualization: The issue of whether newspapers were framing corruption neutrally or negatively (plain areas) or defending and giving a positive view (striped areas).

A conservative newspaper like *ABC* (3rd row) dedicated their entire front page to the PP corruption case, but after the first news proclaimed that "PP must tell the truth about the Bárcenas case,"(*ABC*, 2013) they started defending the actions the PP was taking. As expected, other conservative newspapers (*La Razón*, *La Gaceta*, but not *El Mundo*, which had published the scoop) took a defensive position (Jan. 19-20). It is also worth noting that once *El País* released the excerpts of the parallel financial account (Jan. 31), *La Gaceta*, a far-right newspaper, stopped defending the PP.

I published a blog post about this case study (Rey Mazón, 2013) that garnered a lot of attention in the social media sphere (Twitter). It is worth mentioning that *El Mundo* published a piece[7] on this research: "El Mundo, the newspaper that covers all corruption cases" in a four-column headline. They were interested in showing how the data visualization supported their unbiased work, and redrew the graphic to show *El Mundo* in first place.

In Spain, mass media are usually blamed for maintaining and supporting the bi-partisan system.[8] This time, however, some newspapers were playing a fundamental role in unveiling corruption cases, but most of them only kept reporting about certain corruption scandals. Only a well-informed citizen who escapes the biased point of view of his/her reference newspaper can get the full picture of what is happening and react accordingly.

4. Conclusion

The method for analyzing newspaper front pages that we have described here, as well as the PageOneX.com platform, provide a straightforward way to analyze and visualize news attention to specific stories over time, across or between newspapers. In the future, we imagine either extending this tool or connecting it to others focusing on other media platforms, such as TV[9] and radio broadcasts, or to the online versions of newspapers and social media.

Content analysis, and newspaper content analysis by amount of coverage, has had a long history in the field of communication studies. New tools are enabling novel approaches to this kind of analysis. Some aspects of newspaper content analysis can be automated, some can be distributed (crowd-sourced), some can be done much more quickly by human coders using sophisticated new interfaces. The data produced by such analysis can also be visualized in new ways, and compared against data from other new sources of information flow, such as social media. This essay has explained the approach we have taken with PageOneX, demonstrated its application to several specific stories, and suggested areas for further work. We hope that PageOneX provides a valuable example to anyone interested in monitoring the media: communication scholars, social movement activists, or advocacy organizations.

We invite anyone interested to contact us and to participate in the future development of the platform.

Part of this text is based on the forthcoming article "New Approaches to Newspaper Front Page Analysis," written with Sasha Costanza-Chock.

References

ABC (2013). "El PP debe aclarar la verdad del caso Bárcenas sin medias tintas." *ABC* 18 Jan. Retrieved from http://www.abc.es/historico-opinion/index.asp?ff=20130118&id n=1503988602214.

BIFI, Instituto de Biocomputación y Física de Sistemas Complejos. Universidad de Zaragoza. (2011). "15m." Retrieved from http://15m.bifi.es/tags_full.php.

El País (2013). "Todos los papeles de Bárcenas." *El País* 4 Feb. Retrieved from http://elpais. com/especiales/2013/caso_barcenas/todos_los_papeles.html.

Junta Electoral Provincial de Madrid (18 May 2011). Retrieved from http://numeroteca. org/?p=670.

menéame (2011). "Evolución de la superficie de portada dedicada al movimiento 15M en los periódicos." Retrieved from http://menea.me/r3nm.

Minder, Raphael (2013). "Investigation Shows Spanish Ruling Party's Ex-Treasurer Had $29 Million in Swiss Account." *New York Times* 18 Jan. Retrieved from http://www.nytimes. com/2013/01/19/world/europe/corruption-scandals-widen-in-spain.html?_r=0#p[NtrFhb].

numeroteca. "Superficie dedicada al #15m en portadas de periódicos españoles #nonosva-mos #spanishrevolution http://yfrog.com/gydq0ip." 19 May 2011, 4:05pm. Retrieved from https://twitter.com/numeroteca/status/71350717939585024. Tweet.

Orriols, Lluís (2013). "Corrupción y guerra de trincheras mediática." *El Diario* 1 Feb. Retrieved from http://www.eldiario.es/piedrasdepapel/Corrupcion-guerra-trincheras-mediati-ca_6_96300411.html.

Rey Mazón, Pablo (2011). PageOneX script in Processing. Available at https://github.com/ numeroteca/pageonex-processing.

Rey Mazón, Pablo (2012a). PageOneX. Available at https://github.com/numeroteca/pageonex.

Rey Mazón, Pablo (2012b). Laboratorio visual. Estudios sobre Conflictos y Acción Humanitaria (IECAH). Retrieved from http://www.iecah.org/web/visual/.

Rey Mazón, Pablo (2013). "3 steps to measure corruption coverage in Spain." MIT Center for Civic Media 6 Feb. Retrieved from http://civic.mit.edu/blog/pablo/3-steps-to-measure-the-corruption-coverage-in-spain.

Sánchez, Juan Luis (2011). "Los primeros 40 de Sol." *Periodismo Humano* 26 May. Retrieved from http://periodismohumano.com/temas-destacados/los-primeros-40-de-sol.html.

Suárez, Eduardo (2013). "EL MUNDO, el diario que cubre todos los casos de corrup-ción." *El Mundo* 12 Feb. Retrieved from http://blog.pageonex.com/wp-content/up-loads/2013/02/130212_elmundo_corrupcion-pageonex.pdf.

Varela, Juan (2011). "El #15m de los medios." *Periodistas 21* 11 May. Retrieved from http://www.periodistas21.com/2011/05/el-15m-de-los-medios.html.

Wikipedia (2013). Anexo: Casos de corrupción política en España. Retrieved from http://es.wikipedia.org/wiki/Anexo:Casos_de_corrupci%C3%B3n_pol%C3%ADtica_en_Espa%C3%B1a.

yokopina (2011). "Poli nos echa de la puerta del sol acampadasol." *YouTube*. Retrieved from http://youtu.be/_5Vm48Eeb_Y.

---

1 *Democracia Real Ya* was not only the motto, but also the citizen platform to deepen in democratic values; democraciarealya.es.

2 Among other locations: 20,000 people in Madrid; 15,000 people in Barcelona. *See El País*, "La manifestación de 'indignados' reúne a varios miles de personas en toda España," 15 May 2011 http://www.elpais.com/articulo/espana/manifestacion/indignados/reune/varios/miles/personas/toda/Espana/elpepuesp/20110515elpepunac_12/Tes; *ABC*, Varios miles de «indignados» salen a la calle en toda España," 16 May 2011 http://www.abc.es/20110515/espana/abci-democracia-real-manifestaciojn-201105152210.html.

3 In reference to the protests in Iceland regarding the financial economic crisis (2009), see http://www.guardian.co.uk/world/2008/dec/01/iceland; http://articles.cnn.com/2009-01-26/world/iceland.government_1_prime-minister-geir-haarde-coalition-government-president-olafur-ragnar-grimsson?_s=PM:WORLD.

4 *#NoLesVotes* (Do not vote for them) was the hashtag used in Twitter to promote this cyber movement. First used against the "Ley Sinde" law (Ley de Economía Sostenible [Sustainable Economy Law], March 2011), which opened the possibility of Internet censorship. That led to a second stage of the online movement that urged a change in the electoral system to fight bipartisanship, "Do not vote for them" was their motto, referring to the parties that approved the law. "Les" also meant "Ley de Economía Sostenible."

5 Started in Madrid in February 2011, "Youth without a future" is a citizens' platform to address the problems of the precarious situation of the youth during the economic crisis; juventudsinfuturo.net.

6 Started in Madrid in 2003 during that year's real estate bubble, "Right to housing" is a citizens' platform to address housing problems; viviendadigna.org.

7 "A study by the prestigious MIT in the US shows that this newspaper (*El Mundo*) stands out in the Spanish press for investigating the political parties without exception" (see Suárez, 2013)

8 PP-PSOE, both parties are the ones entangled in more corruption cases; check the Corruptodromo map: http://wiki.nolesvotes.org/wiki/Corrupt%C3%B3dromo.

9 Archive.org is making the TV searchable by recording TV images and captions in a public archive. http://archive.org/details/tv

Accountability Tech — Tools for Internal Activism

Leonardo Bonanni

Sourcemap started out as an activist project; today we sell enterprise software. The goal has always been the same: to understand and improve the way things are made. Today, products can be made in incredibly complicated ways, crisscrossing the globe, inflicting unknown—sometimes unknowable—social and environmental impact. I thought consumers should be able to know what products they are buying, where they come from, and how they impact the world. We should know the carbon footprint of products, and make informed decisions, such as when to buy something locally (to save on shipping) or from far away (where it could be more efficiently produced). And when we buy something, we should be able to connect directly with the people who made it.

That's how Sourcemap began: as a free, crowd-sourced directory of products, their supply chains, and their impact. Researchers, NGOs, and generally curious people could register for free and contribute to the growing database. It was my PhD project at the MIT Media Lab, and my colleagues liked it—as an activist platform. All but one: Bill Mitchell, the former Dean of the Architecture Department and my thesis reader. He also saw Sourcemap as an activist platform—but for a different kind of activist. He told me it would be most useful to *internal activists*: employees who advocate for change from within their companies. After all, there are plenty of people inside companies who want to make the world a better place, and they need tools to make the business case. (Bill suggested I add a button to 'Export to PowerPoint'). In many cases, the impact of internal activists is far greater, since they know more about exactly how things are made, and they have control over what should be made and how.

Making Sourcemap into a tool for internal activism transformed the project from a consumer website into an enterprise platform. I found that while consumers *have the right to know* where products come from, companies *need to know*. After Foxconn and Fukushima, companies began scrambling to find out exactly where their raw materials come from, to avoid running out of critical components, to maintain quality, and to avoid PR disasters. Using the know-how developed to crowd-source supply chain data from the public, we developed a powerful social network that companies use to collaborate with their own suppliers. Today's it's used by major manufacturers to account for all the risks of the supply chain—from traditional metrics like inventories and lead times to the social, environmental, and climate costs of business. In a world this interconnected, accountability is no longer an option. Our task is to make it useful.

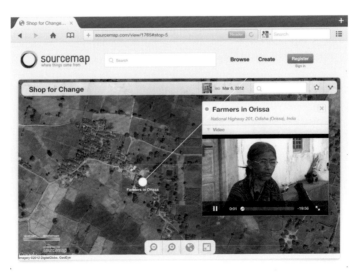

Examples of supply chain maps. Source: sourcemap.com

Fighting Corruption Where and When It Happens — Ambient Accountability

Dieter Zinnbauer[1]

Corruption matters [profoundly and dramatically][2] typically unfold as situated transactions [unsurprisingly, yet surprisingly seldom explicitly recognised] and are highly contingent on context, informational environment, institutional embedding, as well as the dispositions and mutual expectations of the actors involved [all these drivers are increasingly better understood, but not yet fully considered in anti-corruption strategies].[3]

This, in a nutshell, is my guiding proposition for this essay, and this the very particular prism through which I explore the intersection of technology, information and space, and the many exciting opportunities that this cross-over affords for tackling corruption and enhancing accountability in very practical ways.

Enter Ambient Accountability

I anchor this inquiry in a shorthand concept of "ambient accountability", big words for a rather simple idea: How can we shape, use and systematically engage with the built environment and public places and the ways people experience and interact in them, in order to further transparency, accountability and integrity of public authorities and services?[4]

This is a deliberately broad definition and it is entirely technology-agnostic, in order to not constrain the scope of inquiry and to be able to accommodate a wide range of interventions. The concept provides a fresh perspective in at least two important respects:

– On the "fighting corruption side" to think about accountability mechanisms as strategic spatial interventions that empower people right at the place, right at the time when they have to deal with potentially corrupt public officials and service providers, or when they happen to pass by project sites or institutions where corruption issues may surface, a perspective that so far has not been considered prominently yet.[5]

– On the "urbanism and technology side" to direct attention to the little explored, yet very important area of accountability, targeted transparency and anti-corruption that can provide a vast new space for creative exploration and action for all those smart city, urban computing, open government or urban interventionism initiatives that are eager to expand the range of practical applications for their capabilities, creativity and energy.

A first example for ambient accountability that may come to mind is the many anti-corruption campaigns, for example, that often include exhortatory messages prominently displayed on large billboards.

Anti-corruption message, Uganda
☺ futureatlas.com

As important as these interventions might be, they do not provide specific information that is targeted to a particular transaction or exchange and enables citizens to hold public officials to account.

Getting to the Point

So what would then count as ambient accountability in the sense of more targeted information interventions? The following typology might help to identify some good examples and begin imagining new ones. It distinguishes between three interlinked clusters of targeted ambient accountability mechanisms that relate to the three key types of information that citizens require, in order to hold public officials effectively to account: information on what should happen, information on what is actually happening, and information on how to effectively complain when the "ought" and "is" do not match.[6]

A: What Ought to Happen/What Can I Expect? Ambient Accountability to Help Understand Rights, Entitlements and Commitments

This cluster includes measures that equip citizens with information on their rights and entitlements, on what conduct and service levels they ought to expect, and what the terms of exchange should be like. And it is about using the built environment to provide this vital information right where and when you, as a citizen, need it, rather than in some repository of legal texts or online on a website.

One example is tactics to put basic human rights principles related to police detention and search on a billboard and display them vis-à-vis a police station or in a neighbourhood that is subject to a high number of police interventions. The right to know movement, for instance, has worked with graffiti artists and produced some very interesting examples of this type of ambient accountability.

New York, Bronx
Photo: Garrett Ziegler, mural by Dasic Fernández

The information presented can also relate very specifically to a particular transaction. Think about how to figure out your rights when you are in a foreign city and your plane gets cancelled or you want to enter a taxi.

A start, but not all too specific and helpful…   …a much more targeted and empowering
airport display, Brazil. ☺ Dieter Zinnbauer   placard in a taxi, Italy. ☺Dieter Zinnbauer

And ambient information on what should be can also pertain to specific public project characteristics (timeline, budget and completion milestones, etc.—think of your tax dollars at work).

Finally, ambient accountability information on what should be could relate to specific service quality commitments.

B: What Is Going On? Ambient Accountability as Facilitating the Monitoring and Tracking of Performance

Having equipped citizens with all the required information on what to demand and expect, this second main cluster of ambient accountability is now about facilitating the monitoring and understanding of what is actually going on.

Is Watching through Seeing Reversing the Panopticon?

In a very basic, literal sense, this includes deliberate interventions through architecture, design and even just the practical physical organisation of work and service provision in ways that make them more visible and transparent. There is a long history of thinking about public space and social control, starting with Bentham's infamous panopticon. Ambient accountability, however, seeks to turn the table and basically envision a panopticon in reverse. Instead of devising more effective spatial interventions for the state to control its citizens, it seeks to make it easier for citizens to watch the state, its inner workings and performance.

Peepholes on construction site, Toronto, Canada. © Fred Sztabinski

Moscow subway police: a first initiative to use more windows and glass for holding cells to make police work more visible to passers-by and address frequent complaints about abuse. © TI Russia

This train of thought leads directly to the treatment of transparency in architecture as a treasure trove of ideas, thinking and practical applications, and in many ways a journey to the essential roots of transparency that, in its original, pre-political meaning, refers to the material through the quality of objects and substances. There is a rich tradition in public building architecture that uses transparency as a central design principle to embody an optimistic aspiration of enlightened citizenship or communicate a democratic, inclusive vision of government. However, with the ubiquitous use of transparent materials in public and private buildings alike, from glass domes for parliaments to entire glass façades for financial centres, this tradition has become an ever more empty symbolic gesture.[7] It has somewhat lost its focus on practical applications to enhance transparency and accountability in meaningful ways, an ambition that might be worth revitalising to envision new applications in this area. Yet, being able to watch does not necessarily mean being able to understand. Designing the built environment for transparency is just one possible strategy of ambient account-ability to make performance more visible. Pure play design interventions reach their limits when the activities to be disclosed are complex or less tangible.

Displaying Performance/Outcome Where It Happens or Responsibility Resides

But design can be coupled with targeted information interventions that help commu-nicate and understand "what is going on", how well a specific service, project, official or even policy is working.

One area where performance displays have been used sporadically is worker safety.

Site safety performance board, Hong Kong
© Foluisongee

But this is just the beginning. Many other application areas and creative realisa-tions are imaginable. Consider, for instance, this example from Russia, where unful-filled promises to upgrade city streets have led local artists to paint caricatures of responsible politicians around potholes, a strategy that, according to media reports, has been very effective, leading to swift action to fix the streets.[8]

And such ambient performance displays need not be confined to tangible projects and project sites. They can also be used to display the degree of impact of policies where this impact (or a lack thereof) directly unfolds, such as the (non)impact of clean air policies for urban centres.

Air quality display board, Spain

Being presented with performance information at the point of responsibility or intended impact does not only make it easier for citizens who happen to pass by a project site or come to see a public official to spot poor performance and demand reasons for it. In an important psychological twist, it also plays the performance met-rics directly back to those meant to perform or carry broader responsibility for per-formance.

Posting, subway station, New York
ⓒ Dieter Zinnbauer

Public bathroom, airport, Seoul, South Korea
ⓒ Dieter Zinnbauer

C: What Is to Be Done If Things Go Wrong? Ambient Accountability as Facilitating Recourse to Remedial Action in Case of Improper Conduct

To complete the information-to-accountability transmission chain, information on what ought to happen and what actually happens needs to be complemented by information on how to take action, in case of corruption or failing performance.

To do so effectively requires two things: to be able to clearly identify the object, case or transaction that is subject to the complaint, as well as the public official who is involved and/or responsible, so that information can, in many cases, be provided directly on location.

Once direct or supervisory responsibilities are identified, the second ingredient for effective reporting requires an easy way to register complaints. Again, simple ambient accountability interventions can help to advertise such a complaints channel and equip citizens with this vital information exactly when and where they need it. Several systems are in place in a variety of countries to provide information on complaints' mechanisms. One of the best known examples is the unified 311 administrative number for any questions and complaints.

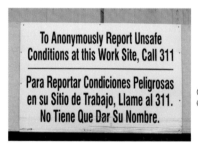

Construction site, bilingual display, New York
ⓒ Leo Reynolds

Such information interventions that work through the built environment are very flexible in their deployment. They can be linked to immovable objects (such as construction sites), spaces in which services are experienced (the toilet example), but also to mobile objects that are encountered only in passing. The best known example for the latter is the increasing use of *How Is My Driving?* schemes for private fleet operators, as well as for more and more public ones.

What makes this example particularly interesting is the fact that this seems to be about the only scheme whose efficacy has been more comprehensively assessed. And the results bode well for ambient accountability: Using *How Is My Driving?* has proven to reduce accident rates significantly, leading insurance companies to offer large reductions in premiums for fleet operators when they put such systems in place. Interestingly, the observed impact does not even depend on large call volumes (which, as most related studies find, are fairly low), but is brought about by the disciplining effect this scheme has for drivers.[9]

The key to the success of all these reporting schemes, however, is a set of functioning and trusted institutional "back-office" mechanisms that give people the confidence that their complaints are attended to confidentiality, as well as effectively.

Why Ambient Accountability Might Just Work …

Insights from a variety of disciplines and fields suggest that ambient accountability has a great potential to make an impact on corruption.

It is fully in line with what we know about when and how information interventions work for effective accountability

On a macro-level it has been clear for quite some time that more transparency in a specific country typically correlates with lower levels of corruption.[10] More recently, field experiments and case studies have begun to shed more light on what is behind this. These studies confirm, for example, that better information about bureaucratic procedures reduces the likelihood that corruption will take place[11]; that gathering and publishing citizen feedback can lead to a step change in public service performance; disclosing local government performance ratings can enhance the trust in government[12], or that publicising central government education payments to local institutions can reduce the leakages and losses from corruption dramatically.[13] What's more, studies also show that such benefits from transparency can also accrue to the less influential and powerful in deeply hierarchical and unequal settings and, importantly, they also point to the fact that overall impact may depend on the information disclosed being very targeted and strategic.[14] All of this bodes well for the potential of ambient accountability as a set of mechanisms that supports very targeted information interventions.

It is immensely norm-promoting

From a psychological perspective, ambient accountability can plausibly expect to be immensely *norm-promoting* because of its immediacy, specificity and direct injection into a social exchange situation. Ambient accountability can therefore be expected to enhance the salience of the expected behaviour and thus support compliance.[15] From an institutional perspective, it is designed to target and directly influence the behaviour of the potential corruptor and the corrupted, and might thus introduce the very element of uncertainty about the other person's behaviour that is required to alter individual behaviours and swing the outcome in an corrupt exchange that sociologists and economists often describe as a delicate bargaining situation greatly influenced by norms and mutual expectations.[16]

It acts as 'calm technology'

From a communication technology perspective, it is also interesting to note that common to all these forms of ambient accountability is an aspect of unobtrusive "information push" and a certain degree of unsolicited information exposure and quasi serendipity.

Citizens may not expect to receive information about their rights or be supplied with information about the real impact of a government policy when passing through a physical space where this policy "happens".

Integration into the built environment means that information is being communicated without people having necessarily to actively search for it. They happen to be exposed to it when being present at a certain place. As long as they might not have an immediate need to use the information and look closely, they may not even become consciously aware of it.

But from a cognitive perspective, the information is held in stock in a peripheral fashion and it can be brought to the fore and linked to action when needed.

Technology experts and cognitive scientists refer to the peripheral qualities of what some of them have called "calm technologies", the provision of information in the background that can be called upon by the individual on a needs basis.[17]

It also works in contexts of information (over)saturation and dispersed responsibilities

The collocation of easy-to-understand performance metrics on policy performance and outcomes can help reduce the feeling of helplessness and confusion that stymies political engagement in the face of an impenetrable thicket of institutions and complex, interconnected political and economic systems.

Restoring the adjacency between entitlements/promises and actual behaviour/performance is a simple mechanism to reverse some of the analytical, informational and organisational difficulties to identify who is causing or responsible for what, and how to confront the ultimate decision-makers with the outcomes of their performance. This means the practical possibility to hold someone to account is at least partly restored in the face of a numbingly complex, networked world that quickly frustrates individual engagement. In addition, ambient accountability corresponds with the notion of the monitorial citizen, a more realistic conception of the possibilities for politically active citizenship in information- and media-saturated environments. These citizens cannot be expected to be "always on" and single-handedly review, digest and act upon the deluge of political information that is being provided to him and her. Instead, monitorial citizens simply scan the information horizon and are ready to engage when alerted by trusted intermediary information brokers or confronted with a particular situation where the information is needed.[18]

Where to Go Next?

As the few examples included in this exploration already indicate: Ambient accountability is an extremely elastic concept that stretches from low-tech stickers to high tech urban screens, from formal official information communiqués to creative artistic interventions. Common to all these approaches, however, are two big shortcomings:

- There is almost no systematic research on what works and what does not under what circumstances.

- There is no real effort underway yet to link what we have learnt about how corruption works, where the hotspots are, and how to fight it, to the immensely rich and diverse expertise, experience and visionary creativity of architects, designers, urban interventionists and situated technology experts.

So, there is ample potential for new ideas, action research, experiments and novel collaborations around ambient accountability initiatives. Here are just two (out of many) of the most promising avenues for further exploration on the more technology-oriented side of things:

Mixing Low and High Tech, Virtual with Meatspace

Ambient accountability is located, publically and "physically", literally hard-wired into a public space, highly visible not only to the directly affected, actively searching and already interested, but also open to chance encounters, to serendipitous encounters with others that just so happen to pass by. This physical and serendipitous quality stands in contrast to the more fleeting and ephemeral nature of initiatives that primarily take place in cyberspace.

Of course, this is a very simplistic, dichotomous view that ignores the many ways that virtual and physical conditions shape each other, but it still flags some important tendencies. Ambient accountability provides a galvanizing concept to tap into the synergies between physical and online more strategically, and envision the information bridges, gateways and outlets that combine the best of both worlds—symbolic, difficult to ignore physical presence and serendipitous exposure with the agility, flexibility and scalability of online information generation and communication. Some popular visions of augmented reality may come to mind as a more futuristic, yet not all too distant notion of this. Think, for example, of a geo-coded rights and accountability information layer for an initiative such as Google's Glass project.[19]

Yet numerous, more simple, mixed-media ideas that also provide for related bridging functions are already being experimented with. These include a wide range of mobile apps that support citizens or service users to monitor public conduct and performance, document and communicate misconduct in geo-aware formats.[20] Furthermore, there are many virtual-physical crossover projects including QR stencils or tags that provide situated links to online information or the many playful initiatives that seek to reproduce popular online aesthetics and digital information in the physical world.[21]

And the growing number of ever cheaper and more powerful, large-scale digital outdoor screens do not only provide a literal window into digital marketing content, but are already being successfully deployed for real-time public interest purposes, including traffic alerts or requests to assist law enforcement in tracking down fugitives. In the US, the latter has been carried out with considerable success. According to industry data, the apprehension of dozens of fugitives is linked to information communicated through large, public digital displays.[22]

FBI alert on digital outdoor screen, US
© OAAA

One may take issue with this Big Brother-like use of digital screens, but it attests to the fact that people do pay attention to and act upon information communicated through such screens, which bodes well for thinking in a much more citizen-focussed manner about other types of accountability information that could be displayed and help citizens better understand and monitor their governments in specific settings.

Crossing FOI with DIY

Many examples of ambient accountability mentioned so far already indicate that this is not just about information provided top-down by the authorities (the freedom of information approach). Ambient accountability also includes a vast array of situated interventions that are driven and work with content generated by citizens, artists and NGOs.

Several NGO initiatives aim at equipping citizens with detailed information at the site of a public service transaction. The Transparency International (TI) group in Lebanon, for example, compiled information on how to secure a building permit, a transaction that is highly vulnerable to corruption, in a brochure and, with the help of the respective ministry, made it available on the premises of the related office. Similarly, the TI group in Bangladesh has provided hospital patients with information on services and prices of medicines outside the hospital, while TI Zambia produced a number of "how-to" posters that describe procedures to get a passport, driver license, etc., for display close to the respective service sites.

Thinking from an ambient accountability about such bottom-up intervention perspectives opens a vast space for new initiatives and experimentation, both in terms of the content to be interspersed into the built environment, as well as the intervention methods available.

Projections and laser-tagging, for example, provide an extremely effective way to target information onto specific objects in the built environment and link the accountability information and messages directly to a specific institution in a very effective, publicity-generating way.

Laser graffiti, Rotterdam, Holland
© Theo Watson

Free Ai Weiwei projections onto Hong Kong police station. © Cpak Ming

Ultimately, however, the greatest, longer-term potential of ambient accountability could be related to presenting real-time, user-generated content and feedback back to the public institution or service provider for an unprecedented level of instantaneous transparency and reflection in feedback mechanisms.

Twitter walls that show real-time mobile messaging feeds can help experiment with a completely new quality of direct, instantaneous feedback and reflexivity.

These types of technologies not only pave the way for displaying tweets, but also linking in other anti-corruption hotline and reporting data, as well as citizen feedback on service performance, policy outcomes, etc., and projecting this information right back on site in plain view not only of the officials and service providers being commented on, but other customers and passers-by as well. The motivating and mobilising impact that comes with such a public display of the accumulated disgruntlement with corrupt behaviour is potentially enormous and may help individual citizens to realise that they are not alone with their complaints, and that many others are equally frustrated and are starting to speak up.[23] Such ambient feedback interventions need not be high tech, however. They can, for instance, also consist of "dialogue boards" in a courthouse that present client feedback, as has, for example, been tried out in Kenya.[24] What's more, there is no reason why one could not try to convince public officials that want to champion the integrity, transparency and customer-responsiveness of their institutions to erect such user feedback displays on site, both to hold the mirror up to their own employees and to gain a political edge over less progressive municipalities elsewhere.

Twitter wall to protest unsustainable palm oil use outside corporate headquarters, Frankfurt, Germany. © Greenpeace

All this is just a start and only begins to hint at what could be explored through the prism of "ambient accountability". Add to this the dramatically expanding opportunities that come with continuous innovation on social media applications, location-sensitive technologies, social discovery mechanisms, the explosion of data related to the "Internet of Things" (a computing concept involving everyday physical objects being connected to the Internet and communicating autonomously) and various open government and DIY data initiatives all increasingly available on ever more powerful mobile devices. Against this backdrop, the field for idea generation and experimentation to use ambient accountability interventions to help citizens organise, protest and actively resist against corruption seem limitless.[25] It is high time to get started.

1 Dieter Zinnbauer (PhD) works on emerging policy issues for Transparency International. This article presents the personal opinion of the author and does not necessarily reflect the views of Transparency International.

2 Just to flag some headline numbers: In opinion surveys, corruption consistently ranks alongside climate change, terrorism and employment as one of the most pressing global issues. An estimated 20 to 40 percent of public budgets and aid are being lost to corruption in developing countries. One in four respondents to a representative household survey in more than 80 countries reports having been asked for bribes when interacting with public services ranging from health and education to police or tax authorities, a portion that rises to more than half of all respondents in several countries including India (Transparency International (2011): Global Corruption Barometer 2010/11; and various reports from the annual Transparency International Global Corruption Report series (http://www.transparency.org/research/gcr).

3 See footnote 16.

4 Some organisational development strategists use the expression "ambient accountability" to describe the incentivising and disciplining impact of peer pressure that comes with lateral, open forms of collaboration.

5 For some innovative thinking from the perspective of crime prevention, see Aiden Sidebottom (2010): "Enriching Corruption: Some suggestions on how situational crime prevention can inform the analysis and prevention of corruption", paper submitted to 2010 ACRN young researchers competition.

6 What follows are just a small number of examples for each cluster, purely for illustrative purposes. For many more examples and a much more comprehensive mapping and discussion, see a related working paper: Dieter Zinnbauer (2012), "Ambient Accountability: Fighting Corruption When and Where it Happens," *Social Science Research Network*, http://ssrn.com/abstract=2168063.

7 For an excellent overview of the role and evolution of transparency as an architectural principle, see Christian Teckert (2008), "Sprünge im Glas. Transparenz—Strategien der Sichtbarkeit in der Architektur," *UmBau 24—Strategien der Transparenz. Zwischen Emanzipation und Kontrolle*, ed. Österreichische Gesellschaft für Architektur (Salzburg: Verlag Anton Pustet).

8 "How Graffiti Made Russian Officials Do Their Job," *redhotrussia.com*, 24 July 2012, http://redhotrussia.com/yekaterinburg-road-graffiti/.

9 For a discussion of related studies, see Lior Strahilevitz (2006), "'How's My Driving?' for Everyone (and Everything?)," *Public Law and Legal Theory Working Paper No. 125* (Chicago: University of Chicago).

10 For an overview, see, for example, Monika Bauhr and Marcia Grimes (2012), "What Is Government Transparency?" *QoG Working Paper Series 2012:16*, Quality of Government Institute (Gothenburg: University of Gothenburg).

11 Klaus Deininger and Paul Mpuga (2005), "Economic and Welfare Impact of the Abolition of Health User Fees: Evidence from Uganda," *Journal of African Economies*, (14) 1, pp. 55–91.

12 Maria M. Garcia and Joseph J. Capuno (2011), "Trust & Transparency under Decentralization: Evidence from a Field Experiment in the Philippines." Available at http://saopaulo2011.ipsa.org/paper/trust-transparency-under-decentralization-evidence-field-experiment-philippines.

13 Ritva Reinikka and Jakob Svensson (2004), "The power of information: evidence from a newspaper campaign to reduce capture," *Policy Research Working Paper Series 3239* (Washington, DC: The World Bank).

14 Leonid Peisakhin and Paul Pinto (2010), "Is Transparency an Effective Anti-Corruption Strategy? Evidence from a Field Experiment in India," *Regulation & Governance* , (4) 3, pp. 261–280.

15 See Celia Moore (2009), "Psychological Processes in Organizational Corruption," ed. David De Cremer, *Psychological Perspectives on Ethical Behaviour and Decision Making* (Charlotte, NC: Information Age Publishing), pp. 35–71.

16 Experiments in corruption research indicate that corrupt or non-corrupt outcomes for a specific social exchange situation are highly contingent on design variations that change expectations and the degree of trust of the participants. See Johann Graf Lambsdorff (2008), *The Institutional Economics of Corruption and Reform* (Cambridge UK: Cambridge University Press).

17 See Mark Weiser and John Seely Brown (1997), "The Coming Age of Calm Technology," eds. Peter J. Denning and Robert M. Metcalfe, *Beyond Calculation: The Next Fifty Years of Computing* (New York: Copernicus), pp. 75–85.

18 Michael Schudson (1998), "Changing Concepts of Democracy," *MIT Communications Forum*. Available at http://web.mit.edu/comm-forum/papers/schudson.html.

19 See http://www.youtube.com/watch?v=9c6W4CCU9M4; for influential discussions of future scenarios for information technologies in urban environments; see, for example, Adam Greenfield and Mark Shepard (2007), *Urban Computing and Its Discontents, Situated Technologies Pamphlet No. 1* (New York: The Architectural League of New York); Mark Shepard (ed.) (2011), *The Sentient City: Ubiquitous Computing, Architecture, and the Future of Urban Space* (Cambridge, MA: The MIT Press).

20 See, for example, "Stop-and-frisk-watch," released by the New York Civil Liberties Union or http://www.nyclu.org/app.

21 See, for example, Aram Bartholl's *Dead Drop* or *Map* projects, http://datenform.de/.

22 http://www.oaaa.org/legislativeandregulatory/digital/aboutdigitalbillboardtechnology.aspx

23 Social movement theories have long recognised this powerful mobilising effect when individuals become aware that a particular problem is widely shared, thus correcting what is often called a general error of attribution. See Doug McAdam, John D. McCarthy et al. (1996), "Introduction," eds. Doug McAdam, John D. McCarthy et al., *Comparative Perspectives on Social Movements* (Cambridge UK: Cambridge University Press), pp.1–20.
For a direct application of this argument with regard to the Internet and political mobilisation, see Clay Shirky (2009), *Here Comes Everybody: The Power of Organizing without Organizations* (New York: Penguin).

24 Barry Walsh (2010), *In Search of Success: Case Studies in Justice Sector Development in Sub-Saharan Africa* (Washington, DC: World Bank).

25 For influential discussions of future scenarios for information technologies in urban environments, see Adam Greenfield and Mark Shepard (2007), *Urban Computing and Its Discontents, Situated Technologies Pamphlet No. 1* (New York: The Architectural League of New York); Mark Shepard (ed.) (2011), *The Sentient City: Ubiquitous Computing, Architecture, and the Future of Urban Space* (Cambridge, MA: The MIT Press).

Political Read-Write Culture and the Logic of Collective Action

Dietmar Offenhuber in Conversation with Lawrence Lessig

Many people know you as the expert on copyright and the creative culture of the Internet. Recently, you have shifted your attention to the corruption of the American political system. In One Way Forward *you coin the term of a "political read-write culture." Could you please explain this term and how it relates to the digital culture of the Internet?*

Well, I guess the point that was so central to the later part of my work on copyright was the way in which technologies were reviving a pattern of cultural production, which was very familiar in the history of culture from the beginning of time until the 20th century. And that pattern was that more people participated in the production and spread of culture. There were professionals, but people also felt empowered to consume, and then to reproduce, and then to modify, and to adjust culture as they incorporated it into their lives. The 20th century was marked by the rise of technologies that made it either unnecessary or embarrassing to engage in that kind of cultural production. Why would you sing and play piano when you could just play the same music by some professional? So we have this period where the basic motif was "shut up and listen" and people learned how to do that. I think there is a similar pattern in the context of politics: The big trick in the 19th century American political tradition was to bring more people into the business of engaging, and bring out more people from one side than the other. And a lot of that activity was the sort of thing that we think as corrupted, like patronage and the way in which bosses use money in the context of bringing people in. But the fact was that politics was about people spreading ideas from themselves to other people. Not broadcasters broadcasting a political message. I think the 20th century produced the same dynamic that exists with culture—that politics is increasingly a very professional enterprise where the data tells the campaigns what they need to say, and they want to control and regulate the spread of that in a very effective and direct way. So, it's once again "shut up and listen"—we got our commercials, don't question that. What was interesting in the beginning of the new version of politics—Howard Dean[1] is the real launch of that—Dean's was the first campaign where the campaign manager Joe Trippi did not control what people did with the message. It was like: Become a supporter of Howard Dean and tell people why in your own way. He tried to encourage a thousand different campaigns on them, and they really believed in the idea of decentralizing control. And that, I think, is the first birth of the idea that—wow, we bring more people into the campaign, and that makes it a more powerful campaign—and then Obama copied that fundraising model, and we began to see iteration after iteration, more sophisticated efforts to do exactly that. That is, it seems to me, read-write politics, and it competes favorably with read-only politics.

Thinking of practices such as hashtag hijacking, isn't there also a danger that such a strategy might backfire by giving up control over the "message"?

Yes, freedom is always messy like this, and I think the dynamic is unavoidable—it is also authentic. Freedom is dangerous, but it is also authentic. I think the Clinton vs. Obama campaign brought this up most dramatically. The perception of the Obama 2008 campaign was that it was freer and more authentic. There was a wider range of people genuinely stepping up and trying to do something. And the Clinton campaign was very heavily choreographed. And the passion that she was able to inspire through this choreography was just an order of magnitude less than the passion Obama was able to inspire. So I think the more sophisticated managers of the future will look at it and say, "Well, there is a tradeoff: We can either have a timid crowd that reliably sends in $20 checks and shows up on election day, or a more vigorous crowd that is more engaged in spreading the message and rooting for our cause." And I think more people will say: "We want the latter."

Spreading ideas is one thing, but writing laws is another issue. What do you think about a read-write approach applied to the actual process of legislation? In Hamburg, a group of citizens have collaboratively written a transparency law, using the social coding platform GitHub, which is a platform for developing open source software. After the city government failed for many years to establish such a law, the citizen-written law got passed this past summer. This might have had something to do with the local government's fear of the success of the Pirate Party. From your perspective, to what extent can we compare the process of writing legislation to the process of writing open source code?

I think there are certain categories, certain examples where it could be useful. I think the Iceland constitution example (where a bottom-up initiative of citizens re-wrote the constitution of the country with the sanctity of the Icelandic government, described in Lawrence Lessig's book *One Way Forward*[2]) is another example of this. But I am not somebody who thinks that it's going to be a good thing to move to the world where representative democracy has been displaced by a kind of open source or free software model of legislation. The reason for that is that there is some basic political science here. And the basic political science is the logic of collective action. The logic of collective action is that the people whom are most directly affected, even though they are a small minority, will have more interest and more power to direct that collective process than the rest of the people who are the mass majority, who might all be affected, but affected in a very small way. So you need systems, representative systems that filter this in the right way, so you can get to the right answer, even though there is this difference in effect. Take climate change for instance—if we had an open source process for writing laws on climate change, there would never be any climate change legislation, because the people who are affected by that—the oil companies and the coal companies—would be right in the middle of that fight. They would have people on that; every single build would be matched by another edit that would be re-built again. And the rest of us, who are invested in this, will not be invested anywhere close to enough to overcome that kind of energy. Now, you can look at the American government right now and the same point is true, because we allow money to be the proxy for influence, and obviously the money manifests itself in the same way. But if we reformed that political system, I'd be more confident about deliberate bodies coming up with the right answer than I am with a system that imagines laws written by, you know, good souls inevitably overwhelmed by interested souls.

This touches on another issue, the limits of transparency. You have argued that we place too much emphasis on transparency and institutional accountability mechanisms. In the context of campaign finance, you have noted, "transparency normalizes dependency, rather than enables in-dependence." However, there is also the kind of transparency established by platforms such as WikiLeaks or ipaidabribe.com. In what way do the limitations of transparency apply to such bottom-up efforts, and what needs to happen so that the information they produce translates into action and change?

You could say that there are three categories of transparency cases. The government taking government data and making it accessible in a standard format way is transparency and unambiguously good. That ought to, all the time, with every bit of government data that can be released, be subject to privacy and similar concerns—I am all for that. What I criticized in my article in *The New Republic* was the idea that would be a sufficient reform to the corrupting influence of money inside of our political system.[3] In my view it is not a sufficient reform, not even a helpful reform; it is necessary, but the consequence of it is actually making things worse. What we also need to fight for is a more fundamental change to make things better—that's the second category. The WikiLeaks category is a third category, and it's a hard one. I guess my view is that the darknet[4] is inevitable and it's a real and permanent constraint on the ability of government to do certain things, and that's a good thing. The government might think—jeeze, we can't torture because it eventually will come out, and that's terrible. And my answer is no, that's good. The modern self recognizes that the way to deal with a lack of privacy is to live in a way that can survive transparency. Now, as applied to the individual, that is a kind of totalitarian story; as applied to the government, that's fine. I am embarrassed by the extreme response by government to Julian Assange and, in particular, Bradley Manning—which is unbelievable brutality that is really hard to understand relative to what was actually going on there. And I am hopeful that we will have more productive WikiLeaks-like alternatives developed. I am disappointed in the OpenLeaks project, but let's think about other ways in which we can address what is a certain feature of the future, which is not data leaks, which gives you a conception of a leaky faucet... The future is data dumps. And when we have data dumps, we need more responsible institutions to be able to filter through and identify the reliable, important information to be making public and the important information not to be making public—so it doesn't jeopardize lives and destroy the privacy of people who should have a legitimate expectation of privacy.

You often have cases where those two spheres intersect, for example, in a case where an individual complains to the city about the conduct of a neighbor; and this complaint consequently becomes a public record bound to be released to the public...

It is a hard line to draw. The German constitutional tradition, in particular the idea that you can be a murderer, but after 20 years it is not permitted to publish the fact that you were a murderer, is, to an American, really very astonishing—but there it is; their commitment to privacy and the protection of the opportunity of somebody to reform and become a new person is deep and significant. And so I think we have a sense of the importance of protecting privacy for various kinds of reasons. But in the United States we don't protect much individual privacy at all and we have enormous protection for government privacy called secrecy—everything is marked "secret" in the government. There is this great calculation of the government's production of public domain data versus the government's production of secrecy data; and the secrecy data is orders of magnitude more than the public domain data. And so, the pathology that leads to more and more of that happening is obvious and well known and, since Daniel Patrick Moynihan,[5] perfectly well analyzed, but it has not changed; it continues unabated.

In your work, you frequently emphasize the importance of trust as the basis for political systems. One central aspect is the trust of the public in their political institutions, but there is also a different aspect, the difficulties activists face establishing trust in the soundness of the data and evidence they collect. For example, in the prominent Supreme Court cases fought by the environmental movement during the '70s, the establishment of trust in the data that had to be collected on a scientific ground was one of the central battles. Of course this was a different time, but do you think that a "political read-write culture" also brings new strategies for establishing trust in crowd-sourced data? What could these strategies look like?

I think there has been a lot of back and forth in the data.gov domain—where the government releases data, and then there is pushback concerning its credibility or authenticity. I think that takes care of itself in a certain respect. We don't have any effective pushback on the secrecy part, because it would be a crime. It still leaves open a really challenging problem, which is: Data alone is not enough, you need investigative journalism and we have no business model for investigative journalism anymore. So what do we do about that? That is the hardest question. The bottom-up blogger is important and some are obsessive and function like investigative journalists. Good for them, but I increasingly see journalism moving more towards bloggers than bloggers moving more towards journalism.

My last question concerns the spatial aspects of activism. It is, for example, interesting to see that the physical presence in the centers of the cities was so central for the Occupy movement, while the online component was more important for the protests related to the SOPA/PIPA bill. Do physical space and visual presence have a special role in your concept of a political read-write culture? Do you see a strategy that specifically deals with that?

I believe it is good if you can get it, but SOPA/PIPA showed us that you do not necessarily need it. I was really excited by some of the Berlin protests around ACTA, which were really amazing, colorful and surprising. Who could ever imagine there would be public protests about a trade agreement? But here it was. I think it might be an essential part of big protests, but it is hard to build because physical protest requires congruence of interest in space which is not necessarily given, depending on the issue. You know, Occupy movements worked well in big cities where there are a large number of people who are likely able to be participating and contributing, but not so well in villages in Wisconsin. So, depending on the issue, it might be essential or it might just not be possible.

In his paper, Dieter Zinnbauer from Transparency International came up with the concept of ambient accountability; accountability-related information directly offered in a specific public space where it is needed ...

It is a very important idea. If you think about the importance of what we call the MIRANDA rights, you know, when you are arrested, the police have to say to you: "You have the right to remain silent" and so on. That is very much a kind of ambient accountability, because once the policeman says this, it makes it harder for the policeman to violate the rule than before. Not just because the arrested citizen would say, "Hey, you can't do that," but because psychologically it becomes harder for the officer to violate these rights. People always belittle the Google "Don't Be Evil" slogan[6] at the core of their corporate Charta. But I think what that misses is that you can kind of imagine an engineer in the Google meeting saying, "Hey, doesn't this violate our principle?" And you could not imagine this at CISCO, where the engineer would say, "Hey what's that about? That's not our job." So, the very fact of placing it into the meme-space of ideas, I do think has a positive regulatory effect.

1 Howard Dean was the Democratic Governor of Vermont from 1991 to 2002.

2 Lawrence Lessig (2012), *One Way Forward: The Outsider's Guide to Fixing the Republic* (San Francisco: Byliner, Inc.).

3 Lawrence Lessig (2009), "Against Transparency." Available at: http://www.tnr.com/print/article/books-and-arts/against-transparency.

4 Describing anonymous, peer-to-peer networks for sharing information protected from commercial or government surveillance. Darknets are used for dissident political communication, http://en.wikipedia.org/wiki/Darknet_%28file_sharing%29.

5 For further reading, see: Daniel Patrick Moynihan (1998), *Secrecy: The American Experience* (New Haven, CT: Yale University Press).

6 Compare Google's ten corporate principles: http://www.google.com/about/company/philosophy/.

COMPEL

Reflections on a Swarm

PlagDoc and Martin Kotynek

An attempt to describe the lessons learned from GuttenPlag.
Food for thought for future net-based investigation platforms.
A contribution to the discussions about "investigative crowdsourcing."

Dr. Karl-Theodor zu Guttenberg had made it to the top of German politics at the age of 40. Coming from an aristocratic family in Bavaria, he was the Secretary of Defense, the most popular politician in Germany, and many hoped he would be the next Chancellor. But in February 2011, he stumbled and fell. Not over a political or private affair, but over his dissertation. As it turned out, he had copied it in large parts from many different sources. "Abstrus," ("absurd"), as Guttenberg put it. But true. Two weeks after the newspaper *Süddeutsche Zeitung* broke the news on accusations of plagiarism, and two weeks after volunteers on GuttenPlag had started to unearth more and more cases of plagiarism in his dissertation, Guttenberg stepped down. It was the birth of investigative crowdsourcing in Germany and one of the largest crowdsourcing projects worldwide so far, with more than 1,000 volunteers investigating together. The volunteers documented 1,218 cases of plagiarism on 393 pages; they identified 135 different sources such as newspaper articles, scientific papers, speeches, and other texts. Sources included the US Congressional Research Service, the Research Service of the German Parliament, and even an undergraduate's essay. Now, more than one year later, the swarm that made up GuttenPlag has vanished, leaving without a forwarding address. What remains is the insight that volunteers, cooperating by way of the Internet in the investigation of an explosive topic, can unleash a tremendous force. It is no longer just journalists, NGOs, or prosecutors who decide which topics bear more intense scrutiny. Everyone can participate. Together with like-minded people, they can use the Internet to search for the truth. Fukushima, the euro bailout scheme, the delayed and over-budget Berlin Airport—there have been a number of recent issues that could be investigated using an online platform. There are other topics not quite of this scale that could also be looked at by a sort of "investigative crowdsourcing," as we will be calling such online cooperation and collaboration activities.

What Is "Investigative Crowdsourcing"?

An attempt to define the term: Many people investigate a complex topic in a collaborative, self-organized process with a centralized moderation using a web-based platform. Their motivation is drawn from interest in the topic and the desire to provoke changes in society.

We will be using the term "swarm" here to denote the group of volunteers in a crowdsourcing project. This article will attempt to explain that the participants in an investigative crowdsourcing project are not an unstructured mass, but a network of independent individuals.

In order to make it easier for interested persons to start a collaborative, investigative project, we want to describe the lessons learned from the GuttenPlag project. In passing these lessons on, we hope that others can learn from both the errors and the successes of GuttenPlag. Based on these experiences, it is to be hoped that—should one be necessary—another swarm may form and that "investigative crowdsourcing" be seen in the German-speaking world as a mainstream tool for a society striving for enlightenment.

Finally, we want to propose some questions for further debate on the question of how such future investigations can be organized. We welcome your comments and ideas!

1. WHY INVESTIGATE WITH A SWARM?

Because a swarm can, at best, find more information than individuals working alone, or even through a team of journalists. The swarm can achieve more than the sum of the contributions of its individuals.

This was the case with GuttenPlag: Thousands of Internet users working together found more cases of plagiarism than were possible for the editorial staffs of large media entities. It was only through this collaborative effort that it was possible to see the true scope of the case. However, GuttenPlag was never a competitor for the media. The platform complemented and assisted the investigative journalists in their work. This could be the general case for investigative platforms: In situations where professional researchers—editorial staff, NGOs, universities, prosecutors—are unable to probe the depths of a topic, a swarm can provide additional assistance.

One should only undertake such a project if one is willing to be one of the hardest workers. While classical crowdsourcing (such as Amazon's commercial service "Mechanical Turk") is often used in order to delegate drudge work to the cheaper labor available on the Internet, this does not work for investigative topics. The open questions and the complexities of the themes demand interested, accurate, thorough, and competent researchers. An enormous amount of time must be invested in order to coordinate, motivate, and support such a group.

"Investigative crowdsourcing" is more work than traditional crowdsourcing. But for those who dare engage in such a collaborative, net-based investigation, the rewards reaped will surpass those from traditional methods. A larger group of participants also has more resources for seeing an investigation through to the end. This can enable the group to perhaps take a decisive step that would otherwise not occur.

2. WHAT ATTRACTS A SWARM?

One cannot expect that an investigative swarm forms for every open question. There are three reasons why this worked in the case of GuttenPlag:

(1) People were willing to invest their free time in "fighting the good fight" for something that was meaningful for them. Quite a number of the GuttenPlag activists—many from an academic background or themselves graduate students preparing their dissertations—were strongly motivated from their own perspective to collect proof, document the academic injustice, and demonstrate that the doctorate needed to be rescinded. In addition, many people wanted to be a part of such a movement of thousands of online volunteers who were in the process of putting one over on an unsympathetic public figure. This was perhaps not the best of intentions. In some cases, it was probably a bit of both reasons. But the participants were united in the drive to counter the statements of zu Guttenberg[1] and to put public pressure on him.

(2) GuttenPlag worked because the participation threshold for beginners was very low. A digital copy of the thesis was soon found, and people quickly learned how to look for plagiarisms. Many of the plagiarized sources were freely available online. The documentation of a plagiarism only needed a few mouse clicks and a little bit of copy & paste. Just a few minutes of effort and a bit of luck were everything someone needed to be able to document a new plagiarism.

(3) The public interest in this topic was enormous, in particular because of the massive media attention. This interest of the media and the general public gave the participants the feeling of contributing to something important and provided more motivation.

In addition to numerous intermediate reports, the contributors were rewarded with an increase in their own personal competence: They learned strategies for searching and how to categorize the plagiarisms they had found.

This can be transferred to other, more complex topics. Investigation platforms could be offering their participants a deal: We will learn new skills together, perhaps with the help of experts or with collaboratively produced interactive tutorials. In return, they contribute their time and apply this new knowledge to throw light on a particular topic. In this case, not only those who are interested in the topic will be active, but also those who wish to learn something new. For example, people who want to investigate a putative case of financial fraud will join forces with those wanting to learn how to read a balance sheet (and hopefully those who want to do both).

3. WHERE IS THE SWARM HEADED?

GuttenPlag was not an uncontrolled, magically self-organized bunch of peers. Just like a flock of birds that flies south in the fall, the collaborative process was guided by a common goal. There were clear agreements about the purpose, principles, and methods of working in the swarm: We are only documenting, we are not setting out political demands. Everything is checked twice, we do not evaluate anything that is not borne by the data. Everything is discussed in the group.

In order for these agreements to be strictly adhered to and to be communicated to new activists, it was necessary to have a clear manifesto, a kind of dogma, stated on the home page of the investigation platform, as well as moderators. They are the backbone of every undertaking of investigative crowdsourcing. At the same time, they are rare assets. Only a few people in German-speaking countries have experience in organizing knowledge online, in bringing about decisions in online communities, and in resolving conflicts in such teams. Every investigative platform needs as many of them as possible so that the project has someone available 24/7 during its peak times, and to ensure that it does not turn into a ghost town during lulls. Even if a platform is not overrun with people at the beginning, the number and quality of the moderators decides whether a crowdsourcing project will be a success or whether it will end in chaos.

Two such moderators were at GuttenPlag from the beginning: both of the platform's initiators. One was in Germany, one was in the USA—because of the time difference, one of them was always online. Over time, there was a core team of about 20 moderators who were regularly active on the platform. Together with approx. 100 other activists, they made up a sort of "task force" that determined the direction of the work and initiated individual projects.

Anyone could be made a moderator at GuttenPlag once they began sorting out and taking care of the platform's content. If one of the other moderators saw one of the volunteers working dedicatedly on the text, they would be offered administrator status. This would give them added functions such as protecting pages from vandalism, editing protected pages, or blocking troublemakers.

For the most part, the GuttenPlag moderators were tech-savvy people who worked as *Wikipedia* editors, were active in Internet policy discussions at the Chaos Computer Club, or worked as researchers. For investigative platforms looking into other topics, it would be feasible to have moderators coming from far different areas. But it is generally useful if at least some of the moderators have had experience in collaborative projects, online or offline.

Without such moderators, GuttenPlag would have degenerated into chaos. Particularly in the first days, so many people were on the platform that it was only possible to get any work done because of the constant stream of volunteers with experience in open content management systems ("wikis") who helped structure the content at GuttenPlag and cleaned up after the vandalism.

Since it is easier to keep activists on a platform than to recruit new people, it is up to the moderators to lead the swarm, as well as to try and keep the friction within the group to a minimum. In order to lead, the moderators need to know which task currently has the highest priority, what the next step is, how to delegate tasks to volunteers, how to keep people informed of what is happening, and to be able to promptly respond to new volunteers asking, "How can I help?" In order to moderate in a conflict situation, the moderators have to use de-escalation strategies — and have the final word in the extreme case of having to forcibly remove someone from the swarm.

With GuttenPlag, there were a number of times at which the tension in the group created a sort of herd instinct that threatened to spin out of control and split the group. This would have hindered the investigation. It is normal to have conflicts arise in such a situation: One does not see the others face-to-face, the only communication is indirect communication, and misunderstandings thus tend to build up. If moderators want to be able to influence such situations, they need to be constantly active in the project in order to be credible with the swarm.

Just as with many other collaborative processes on the Internet, a chat room was very important for GuttenPlag. This was a real-time communication channel connecting up the volunteers, used alongside the investigative platform. Here it was possible to solve conflicts out of public view. Moderators and the "task force" were able to coordinate with each other and to discuss their problems "live." At GuttenPlag, the activists met in a chat room at appointed times in the evenings to decide what direction the future work was to take. The chat thus proved to be the driving force for a number of initiatives on the platform, enabling the task force to show the other volunteers how to solve particular problems.

Both GuttenPlag and the follow-up platform VroniPlag demonstrated the danger of having a separate chat room. A chasm grows between the volunteers who are only active on the platform, and those who are also active in the chat. This can only be bridged by active communication.

4. THE METHODOLOGY

An investigative platform needs to have the technical basis in order to withstand an onslaught of volunteers. This was not the case at the beginning of GuttenPlag. The project began as an open text document using the Google Docs service. This broke down on the following day, as it could not keep up with the load of interested persons. As soon as about 100 people were working in the document at the same time, it would get flakey. All the persons who were currently editing would be thrown off, or it became painfully slow to use, or the document could not be opened at all.

The swarm moved to a wiki, a web site where anyone can add, edit, or delete pages using a browser. The content management system behind the screen stores information about who changed what [when]. This makes it possible to understand where and how errors occurred and permits the restoration of a previous version. Some individuals, the moderators, have extended rights so that they can delete pages or protect them from vandals.

GuttenPlag chose the California-based company Wikia as its technology provider. The initiators of GuttenPlag felt that it would be able to deal with a large number of readers and editors because it has a very broad technical basis. (In all, over 20,000 different IP addresses edited pages in the wiki. Wikia reported that there had already been more than ten million page views just two weeks after the start of the wiki). The service is free of charge and also permits anonymous volunteers. In addition, the initiators of GuttenPlag trusted the company, since it was founded by the initiator of *Wikipedia*. Wikia took care of the work and costs involved with providing the technology and, in exchange, sold ads to be displayed on the pages.

An additional reason for choosing Wikia was that the servers are physically located in the USA, and are therefore not susceptible to restraining orders or political pressure [from German authorities]. The decision to use a commercial provider for an investigative platform, or to run the server yourself, needs careful consideration. On one's own server one had control of the user interface, the connection to external systems, the content, and the users. This might be a good reason for an investigative platform to remain independent of the infrastructure of institutions such as universities or media companies. That way, no one can stop the project or force it into a particular direction. In addition, one can avoid alienating potential volunteers who would be leery of trusting a particular company or institution.

An investigative platform should also offer its volunteers the technical tools for simplifying the research. For example, having a program that checks the numbers in an income tax declaration for plausibility according to Benford's Law would be advantageous. VroniPlag, the successor to GuttenPlag, has a number of semi-automatic tools that were developed for checking suspicious passages directly with Google or for coloring identical passages in texts.

5. DEALING WITH DESTRUCTIVE ELEMENTS

Whoever starts a research platform must be prepared to deal with people who are attracted to the platform with the intention of provoking failure. GuttenPlag had its share of troublemakers who tried (perhaps motivated by political reasons) to interfere with the search for plagiarism. For example, they would post plausible but false "findings" in the lists. But even people who do not subscribe to the goals of the platform do not necessarily have to be seen as a large problem if these three strategies are observed:

(1) Some people find it important to state their opinions in prominent locations on the Internet, for example, as a comment on articles by news organizations or in blogs. An investigative platform should offer the possibility of commenting, announced on the first page, and easy to reach and be spontaneously used without registration. The forum at GuttenPlag, however, quickly developed into an unmoderated "cesspool" (as it was called amongst the moderators) because no one had the time or capacity to deal with the aggressive and non-constructive comments filling the pages. The ease of use of the forum was found to be satisfactory for the commentators. They could dump their frustrations there without getting in the way of the investigation itself and inhibiting the work process. Maybe it would be possible to moderate such a forum and thus turn a potential "cesspool" into a gold mine. Perhaps the critics can be invited to convince themselves of the utility of the platform and be turned into volunteers.

(2) Moderators constantly have to clean up after vandals who delete content from the platform, insert incorrect information, or—as was the case with Gutten-

Plag—add pages and pages of Bible verses to the lists of potential plagiarisms. The moderators have to delete these entries, or revert them, and sometimes have to resort to blocking the users involved. At least the wiki automatically generates a publically visible list of all the edits so that it can quickly be seen who has just changed what.

(3) Some people want to work with the platform, but are of a different opinion or want to move the platform in a different direction from the majority of the volunteers. Sometimes they act against the decisions of the swarm. Instead of casting them out, it has proved effective at GuttenPlag for a moderator to engage that person in a discussion in a private chat or via e-mail and to forge a compromise. In the case that a volunteer has gone a bit too far, it is easier to accept the criticism in a private communication channel. Often it was discovered in these discussions that it was simply a misunderstanding.

In general: The more moderators there are for keeping everything in order, the less destruction can be caused by individual troublemakers. Deletions and blocking users should only be used in clearly defined situations and only as an ultima ratio. Otherwise the moderators are easy targets for allegations of censorship. Deletions and blockings often serve to escalate conflicts about differences of opinion within the project.

6. DOCUMENTING THE WORK

A bloodthirsty mob, descending on some poor, defenseless creature out of the depths of the anonymous Internet with the goal of publically humiliating him or her—this should not be the impression a swarm leaves behind, and it should not even whisper at such an intention. If the investigative platform follows social values and norms, it should still be possible to permit volunteers to participate without hurdles. Pseudonyms connect with a pre-existing identity on the Internet. Other net-savvy people may already know and trust this pseudonym.

GuttenPlag stood in the crossfire of intense criticism because of the decision not to insist on the use of civil names. In hindsight, this decision was absolutely necessary, as it would have frightened off many people to insist on such names (for example, one volunteer who was named in the media was sent anonymous, threatening letters). But if anonymity is permitted on a research platform, special care must be taken that all of the steps can be retraced and that the volunteers apply ethical and practical guidelines of investigative journalism and science. Evidence must be collected without prejudging the result; no premature condemnations; research must be done in all possible directions; both incriminating and exculpating material must be treated; multiple sources must be used, etc.

For the volunteers at GuttenPlag, it was clear on the basis of the facts that the doctorate needed to be rescinded. It was considered to be the goal of the platform to deliver the proof of these facts. It was not, however, a goal to express political demands for resignation. (There were discussions about this, and drafts of an open letter were made out, but this would have harmed the self-chosen strict objectivity and would have meant that all the volunteers would be forced to share this opinion.)

In the first step, the documentation of the facts, the platform was very cautious—particularly because speculations could be legally dangerous. At the beginning, the documentation registered "textual matching," "peculiarities," and "strong indicators." The assessment of these points as examples of plagiarism was only taken at a later time. This second step, the assessment of the research result, needs to have clear, publicly visible rules so that all of the volunteers can proceed in a like-minded manner. Often the rules are modified as the assessment proceeds. Every assessment needs to be conducted along the lines of the scientific principle of "peer review" with a four-eye-principle. Moderators need to assess samples and make all steps taken reviewable for the general public. The platform needs to undertake all possible steps to defend itself against criticism of the work. As soon as the work is published, the attacks can be massive, so the work needs to be unassailable—any weaknesses in the arguments need to be clearly stated.

The preliminary results need to be made clear to the general public through the use of evaluative wording such as "such an explanation seems improbable because..." or "here we see the pattern clearly." Statements like this make it easier for the media to quote the findings of the platform.

When an intensive documentation and evaluation phase is over, the platform needs to find a good time to close the case (instead of having the project peter out because of time and energy deficits, as was the case with GuttenPlag). A report is, on the one hand, an important contribution to the public discussion of the case. On the other hand, it gives the volunteers a sense of closure. The report should document the methods of research and evaluation used and attempt to summarize and analyze the findings. As in any scientific paper, the report should include open questions and explain the steps that need to be taken so that the volunteers can judge the amount of time needed to continue with this case. The platform, however, should not completely disappear, because at some point in the future new findings may show up, or the older findings can be seen in a new light and thus take on a new meaning.

7. OPEN COMMUNICATION

The barcode used in GuttenPlag was designed to visualize the places in the doctoral thesis of Karl-Theodor zu Guttenberg where plagiarism had been found. Its purpose was to serve as a kind of progress bar and to inform new volunteers as to which parts of the thesis had already been investigated. It turned out, however, to be a good tool for communicating with the general public, because it was intuitively understandable and made a nice illustration for reporting the case in the media. This experience demonstrated that research platforms need to be able to visualize their work and to publish it under as free a license as possible. A good possibility here is the use of the Creative Commons Attribution License. This permits anyone to use the material, as long as the source is named.

It is also a good idea to keep an open channel to mainstream media, press agencies, and specialized blogs from the very beginning. Collaborators in a research platform don't have to feel the need to communicate every finding immediately. But they should communicate openly, in order to build up trust. Journalists often want to have home stories, personalized stories. Research platforms can play along with this to a certain degree, but the facts are what should be in the focus of any story. Exclusive rights to a story weaken the platform's independence and position it as a competitor to the other media players. All serious media should be treated equally. (One does need to respect deadlines—national newspapers often print their first issue in the late afternoon of the previous day, weekly newspapers and magazines often have a deadline one or two days prior to publication).

A press review posted on the platform not only serves to motivate the activists, but it is also good for external people, as it demonstrates the relevance of the work being done by the volunteers.

FOOD FOR THOUGHT

On the basis of the lessons learned at GuttenPlag we, the authors of this text, discussed how "investigative crowdsourcing" could be developed in the German-speaking world so that collaborative research projects such as GuttenPlag, VroniPlag or WulffPlag do not remain singularities. In the following, we formulate our ideas as food for thought—but perhaps we are completely off track with this. We hope that you will be active in contributing your own ideas, objections, and experience reports!

First Idea: A Central Investigation Platform?

We asked ourselves: Would it make sense to set up a central, permanent research platform that would be open to all projects? That would have the advantage that this platform in time would offer a good infrastructure for all sorts of research that would be available to everyone. In and around the platform there would be an experienced and well-coordinated team to develop competency in research over time. They could be an established first point of contact for project ideas. In addition, a solid community would possibly be easier to mobilize than having to set up a new platform for every new case and make it generally known. What would the disadvantages of such a central platform be? How could misuse be avoided? How can it be avoided that the platform falls into disuse? Would individual platforms for each case be better?

Second Idea: A Foundation?

Should "investigative crowdsourcing" be funded by an independent foundation? It could be organized in such a way that the foundation itself does not have a research agenda, so that the individual platforms have a higher respect. It could restrict the funding to solely be for technical and procedural help. The foundation could possibly take care of any donations that might arrive in order to set up a server infrastructure or for developing research tools. Or would such a foundation be in complete opposition to the idea of a swarm? What are the dangers involved in such a pooling of interests?

Third Idea: Symbiosis with Established Media?

What position should a research platform take in relation to mainstream media? What about a symbiosis, a relationship in which both sides profit from cooperation? GuttenPlag was both the target of reporting and the source of information for the media at the same time. The media was important for GuttenPlag as a multiplier bringing in new people who had just heard about the platform. This could be intensified: Media such as the British daily *The Guardian* or the US research organization ProPublica have recognized that outside of their research staff, perhaps even amongst their readers, there are experts for almost every topic imaginable. They are focusing on cooperating with the general public ("Open Journalism").

Is this idea even being discussed in the German-speaking world? Would it even work here that journalists contribute their experience towards the success of a research platform and, in return for their cooperation, obtain better research results than they would working alone? Or should research platforms work independently of media? Is the danger of assimilation perhaps too large? Is there even an individual medium that would be able to get cozy with a critical mass?

Fourth Idea: New Topics?

Which topics would have been interesting for "investigative crowdsourcing" in the past twelve months? Why? Which topics are not even possible for public, collaborative research? Which topics would interest you so much that you would get active in a platform researching that topic? Which topics are the most important ones that would need to be investigated by a swarm?

Reprinted with minor revisions from http://de.guttenplag.wikia.com/wiki/Reflections_on_a_Swarm with kind permission from the authors. First published on June 8, 2012 in German; initial translation by WiseWoman.

This text only reflects the personal opinions of the two authors. It was written on their own initiative, independent of GuttenPlag and their respective employers. It was done on their own time on private computers. All costs incurred, such as travel expenses, were paid for out of their own pockets.

The authors wish to thank Kai Biermann from *ZEIT ONLINE*, Johannes Kuhn from *Süddeutsche.de*, Amanda Michel from *The Guardian*, as well as KayH from GuttenPlag/VroniPlag, for their helpful comments on the drafts of this text.

The initial translator wants to thank Leo and Linguee for the fantastic free tools that ease the translation process.

"Reflections on a Swarm" by PlagDoc and Martin Kotynek is available under a CC-BY 3.0 license (Creative Commons Namensnennung 3.0 Deutschland).

The authors can be contacted by e-mail at investigativescrowdsourcing@googlemail.com and via Twitter at @PlagDoc and @martin_k .

A visualization of the annotated dissertation created by the Guttenplag collective is used as the cover of this volume. The visualization was created and kindly provided by User8.

1 Translator's note: zu Guttenberg stated that the accusations of his dissertation being a plagiarism were "absurd," but that there might be an odd footnote that was amiss, which would be corrected in a second edition.

Crowdsourcing a Street Fight

Aaron Naparstek

As Jan Lee leaned over the car's windshield to take a photo of the dashboard parking permit, a man approached shouting, "Who are you? What are you doing?!"

Lee ignored him and snapped a photo. It was January 27, 2006, Mott Street, New York City, not far from the site of the former World Trade Center. An antique dealer in Lower Manhattan's Chinatown, Lee regularly photographed illegally parked cars around his neighborhood with official-looking placards on their dashboards.

The man hit Lee in the arm, pushing his camera aside. "You can't take pictures!" he shouted. Lee told his attacker to leave him alone or he would call the cops. "I am a cop" the man said as he flashed a badge and pushed Lee up against a metal storefront gate.

The police officer seized Lee's camera, dragged him by the collar to the nearest precinct house and forced him to kneel on the sidewalk for 15 minutes with his hands cuffed behind his back.[1] Eventually, the police let Lee go, but not before instructing him that he needed an official permit from the NYPD to shoot photos of cars belonging to law enforcement personnel. That, of course, is not true. There is no such law in New York City.

—

Chinatown had been particularly hard hit by the terrorist attacks of September 11th. Toxic fires burned for weeks. Streets, telephones, electricity and other vital services were disrupted for months. Reconstruction dragged on for years. It had been a tough time for the local residents and business owners.

But by January 2006, Chinatown had finally, mostly, gotten back to normal—with one glaring exception. Traffic congestion on local streets was still horrible. In the immediate aftermath of September 11th, New York City government had more important things to do than enforce parking regulations against the police, firemen and numerous other government employees and first-responders who had raced to the rescue of Lower Manhattan and kept the city running through the crisis. But four years later, parking regulations still weren't being enforced, and the streets of Lower Manhattan had become a veritable parking lot for the private motor vehicles of government employees.

Cars with government placards on their dashboards could park pretty much wherever they wanted and never have to worry about getting summonsed or towed. In fact, cars didn't even need a placard. A sweatshirt or pad of paper bearing the logo of a government agency or public employees' union would usually suffice. Adding to the problem, it seemed that any government or union office could produce its own "official" parking placards. Though the placards had no actual legal basis, they allowed motorists to park on sidewalks, at unpaid parking meters, in front of fire hydrants—essentially, wherever they wanted. The New York City Police Department's traffic enforcement agents simply refused to put parking tickets on vehicles bearing placards, especially when those cars, more often than not, belonged to employees of the NYPD itself.

More than four years after September 11th, Chinatown's streets were still choking on gridlocked traffic and the locals were sick of it. It was particularly galling that so much of the traffic was caused by government employees. So, Lee and a handful of community members had begun to document the problem and raise awareness. They photographed illegally parked cars with government placards and even produced a short video called *Clogged Arteries* to illustrate how government workers' illegal parking was hurting local businesses and wrecking the neighborhood's quality of life.

Transportation Alternatives (T.A.), New York City's leading advocacy organization for pedestrians and cyclists, was interested in the problem. They commissioned a consultant, Bruce Schaller, to conduct a study of government employee parking in Lower Manhattan. Schaller's findings were remarkable. He estimated that illegally parked government employees in Lower Manhattan cost New York City a whopping $46 million per year in uncollected parking meter revenue. Schaller also found that government employees were twice as likely to drive to work in transit-rich Lower Manhattan as their counterparts in the private sector. If government workers commuted by automobile at the same rate as private sector workers, 19,200 fewer vehicles would enter Lower Manhattan each day. Parking placards, it turned out, were a major source of Lower Manhattan's crushing traffic congestion. As Schaller told Streetsblog.org, the publication I created and launched in the spring of 2006, "Free parking has a tremendous impact on the decision whether to drive or take transit."

The problem extended well beyond Lower Manhattan. Matthew Roth, a staffer at Transportation Alternatives, regularly heard complaints about illegal government parking from all over the city. Around fire houses, police stations, schools and government offices, wherever one found a major concentration of public employees, nearby streets and public spaces were jammed with illegally parked cars with official-looking placards on their dashboards. Chinatown activists weren't the only ones documenting the problem. At community meetings in Downtown Brooklyn, the South Bronx and Long Island City, Queens, Roth heard the same complaints.

Motivated by the grassroots outpouring, T.A. published a second study in the fall of 2006 analyzing the problem citywide and breaking it down by government agency. This study found that New York City police personnel were responsible for 46 percent of the total parking placard abuse, by far the largest share from any single government agency. In other words: The government agency responsible for enforcing the city's parking regulations was, in fact, New York City's most egregious parking scofflaw.

Despite the two T.A. studies, a lot of press coverage and a growing clamor from local community groups and their representatives in City Council, the NYPD refused to respond and Mayor Michael Bloomberg seemed uninterested in addressing the issue. Bruce Schaller's original study suggested a reason why this might be so. In a big, crowded city, on-street parking space is a precious commodity. Though it was never accounted for in public employee unions' contract negotiations, free, on-street parking amounted to a government employee perquisite worth tens of millions of dollars per year. They weren't going to give it up without a fight.

—

In the fall of 2006, Greg Whalin, the Chief Technology Officer of Meetup.com, launched a web site called MyBikeLane.com. A regular bike commuter, Whalin had grown frustrated with all of the cars and trucks he found blocking the bike lanes on his daily commute between his home in Brooklyn and his office in Lower Manhattan. He created MyBikeLane.com in his spare time. It allowed anyone to upload a photo of a bike-lane blocking motorist, write a comment and drop a pin on a Google Map where the incident occurred. The web site kept a running tally of license plate numbers and mapped the exact locations throughout the city where bike lanes were being blocked.

Today, the crowd-sourcing and mapping concepts behind MyBikeLane.com may not seem all that remarkable. But recall what the state-of-the art looked like in the fall of 2006: The iPhone was not yet invented, Facebook had only recently expanded beyond college and high school students, and Google Maps was still smaller than MapQuest. It was the dawn of the Web 2.0 social media era and MyBikeLane.com was an incredibly cool new idea. I wrote about it on Streetsblog and it spread quickly by word-of-mouth.

Whalin's web site gave me an idea: What if we had a MyBikeLane.com for illegally parked government employees? Then all of those people who were showing up at community meetings with stacks of photos of illegally parked cars would have a productive place to put their energy. And in doing so—in compiling all of this information online in one place—we would have a much more comprehensive sense of the problem. I called the project UncivilServants.org.

Greg Whalin agreed to re-purpose his MyBikeLane.com code and build the new site's back-end for free. Matthew Roth and Transportation Alternatives took on the responsibility of maintaining and running the web site. Nick Grossman, Streetsblog's lead developer, shepherded the design and production of the web site and put the pieces together. I insisted upon one particular detail: The button the user clicked to "submit permit abuse" would look like the familiar orange parking ticket that New York City motorists so loathe to find on their windshields. The metaphor would be clear: UncivilServants.org gave citizens the power to hand out virtual parking tickets to government employees.

UncivilServants.org launched on March 15, 2007 and was an immediate hit. Within days the site filled up with hundreds of images and reports of vehicles with government placards demonstrating virtually every imaginable form of illegal parking. Each submission was pinned to a New York City street map and tagged with the name of the government agency listed on the dashboard parking placard. With the click of a pull-down menu, anyone with a web browser and Internet connection could see which neighborhoods suffered the most illegal parking, which government agencies were the biggest perpetrators, and which specific vehicles were the biggest law breakers. A problem that had previously only been visible on a car-by-car, street-by-street basis or through expensive, time-consuming studies by professional transportation consultants, could now be seen in real-time, citywide.

New York City's media loved UncivilServants.org. "Memo to all city employees:" blared the *New York Post*. "New Yorkers are watching to make sure you don't park illegally—and if you do, they'll post a picture of your car on the web." The headline in the *New York Sun* read: "A New Deterrent for Parking Violators: Shame." UncivilServants.org earned widespread coverage, mostly favorable, in the daily newspapers and on television news networks. The media attention drew more submissions to the web site and the web site breathed new life into Transportation Alternatives' campaign to reform New York City government's parking placard system. Advocacy is about drawing attention to an issue and UncivilServants.org was an outstanding attention-getter.

Needless to say, not everyone was thrilled with the new web site. Almost immediately, the comments section at UncivilServants.org heated up into a fierce debate over the online publication of government employees' license plate numbers. Police officers complained it was a potentially dangerous violation of their privacy and harmed their ability to work undercover. "To take pictures of cops' cars with the license plate visible for every skell to see is dangerous," argued one commenter calling himself bklyncop01. "Skell" is police slang for a criminal.

The debate over the publication of government employees' license plate numbers generated yet more press, including coverage in the *New York Times*.[2] In response to

UncivilServants.org, launched in March 2007, was an immediate hit. Within days the site filled up with hundreds of images and reports of vehicles with government placards demonstrating every form of illegal parking. Screenshot courtesy of Transportation Alternatives

the complaints, Transportation Alternatives decided to change the web site's policy. Though it added substantial manual labor, T.A.'s staff would review every submission and blur all license plate numbers before allowing photos to be published on UncivilServants.org.

The policy change was not enough to satisfy angry police officers. At NYPD Rant, an unofficial online discussion forum for New York City police officers, commenters vowed revenge against T.A. staff and New York City cyclists. NYPD Ranters posted photos of Roth and T.A. executive director Paul White along with threats urging fellow police officers to "hammer" them if they saw them on the street.

The threats from police were, in a funny way, a sign of progress. Prior to UncivilServants.org, there had been no dialogue at all. The web site created a space for government employees and the public to talk about the issue and the conversation exposed a profound sense of entitlement. A March 22 comment on UncivilServants. org by an anonymous writer claiming to be a recently retired police officer neatly summed up the attitude behind parking placard abuse:

> I have no intensions [sic] of ever parking legally whenever I am in NYC. It is a perk that has been in standard practice since the end of time... I put my life on the line for the ungreatful [sic] liberal scum of this city and this is how they repay us. Screw you and your whining... I am owed a certain perk... thanks to the brotherhood of blue I am assured that I can park anywhere I want with impunity. Every cop in the city is on the same page. We do not summons our own. Take as many pictures of my auto as you like because I answer to no one.

The online dialogue between government employees and the public was a remarkable new development and comments like these were an embarrassment to city officials. A Streetsblog commenter named Steve described the first few days of discussion on UncivilServants.org. "For the first 48 hours," he wrote:

> The majority of the commentary from law enforcement was veiled and explicit threats of physical violence, irrational emotional appeals based on NYPD and FDNY killed in the line of duty, puerile political attacks on "sissy liberals." ... Gradually the violent and irrational verbal attacks began to recede (they are by

A woman waits to cross the street amid illegally parked government employees' cars at the Bronx County Courthouse, October 11, 2005. Photo: Transportation Alternatives

no means gone), and some rational voices among law enforcement commenters emerged… The overall debate at UncivilServants.org is extraordinary. It could
never take place face to face.

Most significantly, New Yorkers began to see results on their streets. The week after
the launch of UncivilServants.org, Deputy Inspector Gin Yee, the new commanding
officer of Chinatown's Fifth Precinct, ordered the towing of fifteen cars, twelve of
which belonged to fellow NYPD officers. Yee also confiscated the vehicles' parking
placards. After years of complaints and inaction, local merchants were thrilled at the
sudden change in policy. And it wasn't just a one-day show-of-force. In the following
weeks, the Fifth Precinct posted flyers throughout Chinatown and an official memo
circulated, notifying parking placard holders that they would be towed "in response
to Transportation Alternatives' request."

As UncivilServants.org continued to expose parking placard abuse, T.A. kept up
the political pressure. In May 2007, Streetsblog learned that Mayor Bloomberg was
considering comprehensive reform of the city's official parking permit system. That
month he appointed Janette Sadik-Khan as the new commissioner of New York City's
Department of Transportation. Sadik-Khan immediately initiated a study of gov-
ernment-issued parking placards along with a transformative strategic plan called
"Sustainable Streets." In July, Sadik-Khan told reporters that a parking permit "crackdown" was "getting closer."

In October 2007, the *New York Times* editorial page called on Mayor Bloomberg to
"take away parking permits from city employees" and "end the free parking." Chinatown's Fifth Precinct kept up its enforcement, towing placarded vehicles throughout
2007.[18] There were signs that other government agencies were going after illegally
parked employees as well. In August, New York City's Parks Department broadcast a
memo ordering a crackdown on the rampant illegal employee parking in and around
Manhattan's Central Park.

Finally, at a press conference in January 2008, Mayor Bloomberg announced that
City Hall would implement "a comprehensive program to reduce the number and
misuse of government parking placards." He ordered every city agency to reduce its
number of parking placards by at least 20 percent. Additionally, he announced that

only the Police and Transportation Departments would have the authority to issue placards, the NYPD would create a new enforcement unit to ensure compliance, and he put a Deputy Mayor in charge of figuring out the specific parking permit reductions at each city agency.

Union leaders for New York City teachers, firefighters and police officers complained loudly and NYPD Ranters declared, "The war is on." Nevertheless, later that spring, after City Hall's study discovered 142,000 parking permits in use—tens of thousands more than anyone expected—New York City government announced a 32 percent reduction in the number of official parking placards. The biggest cuts, of course, came from the Police Department.

—

Two years after Chinatown merchant Jan Lee was handcuffed and detained for snapping photos of illegally parked government employees, New York City's parking placard system had been reformed. While it is difficult to quantify its specific impact, it is clear that UncivilServants.org was instrumental in helping to bring about the change. T.A. executive director Paul White credits UncivilServants.org for "exposing high-profile abuse, generating major media coverage and giving frustrated citizens access to new levers of power."

UncivilServants.org created accountability where there previously had been none. It did this in a few ways. First, it was a great use of crowdsourcing for advocacy. It gave citizens a productive way to engage in activism at a highly local level to make a meaningful contribution toward solving a citywide problem. Second, UncivilServants.org was an outstanding attention-getter. It made reporters' jobs easy by providing them with a smorgasbord of stories and photos of law-breaking government employees caught in the act. The fact that the web site's map-based crowdsourcing technologies were still relatively novel in 2007 made the story even more compelling. Third, UncivilServants forced a public conversation that had previously been impossible. It created a new space for citizens and government employees to argue and discuss a heated, emotional issue in relative safety, un-mediated by city bureaucrats. Finally, and perhaps most importantly, UncivilServants.org amplified the power of an existing advocacy campaign. It is unlikely that the web site would have worked so well on its own. But with the staff at Transportation Alternatives cultivating and moderating crowd-sourced submissions, spoon-feeding juicy tidbits to the local press and actively lobbying the issue at City Hall, UncivilServants.org was able to generate real impact.

This story, however, does not necessarily have a happy ending. Despite City Hall's 2008 reforms, parking placard abuse is still rampant in New York City. The problem is not solved and T.A.'s campaign is ongoing.

A 2011 study by T.A. found that 24 percent of parking placards are fraudulent or otherwise invalid, and 57 percent of placard holders use their permits to park illegally. As an experiment, Transportation Alternatives recently manufactured its own "official" parking placard for an imaginary government office called "the New York State Numismatic Agency." They stamped the placard with the seal of the Republic of Bulgaria, placed it on the dashboard of a rented Dodge Caliber, and spent an entire day parking in various illegal parking hotspots around New York City. NYPD enforcement agents honored the Bulgarian Numismatic placard. After seven hours of illegal parking, T.A. never received a summons.[3]

In 2011, a Manhattan City Council member named Daniel Garodnick introduced a bill that would require city-issued parking placards to be equipped with a bar code to make it easier for enforcement agents to discern which placards are legitimate. In testimony before City Council, the NYPD said they were opposed to the idea of putting bar codes on parking placards. They argued that only Police Commissioner Ray Kelly should have the power to determine what specific security features and tools are used on official parking placards. Ray Kelly, apparently, does not believe there is any value in making government parking placards machine-readable.

Transportation Alternatives shut down UncivilServants.org in November 2012. Though the site had mostly been inactive for a couple of years, police officers at NYPD Rant noticed.

"WE WON!... WE WON!" declared one NYPD Ranter called Curious George. "UncivilServants.org, you shall not be missed."

Another NYPD Rant commenter named Blue Trumpet replied with a more sobering assessment. "Who won?" he asked. "They did." He continued:

[Look at] the massive restrictions introduced to the entire permit/placard process. This has included the establishment of an Internal Affairs Bureau unit to police the police on this issue, complete with the towing and ticketing of police vehicles violating the extremely restrictive rules that have been introduced. As far as the website being shut down, it basically wasn't needed anymore since they won the war.

UncivilServants.org showed the power of simple, low-cost, web-based technologies to provide citizens with the ability to hold government more accountable. But it also showed the limitations of this technology while giving us a glimpse of the next frontier. While UncivilServants.org was effective in shining a light on a particular form of minor government corruption, generating media attention and ultimately forcing City Hall to change policy, the web site had no actual legal enforcement power. The biggest abusers of parking placards—the NYPD—are still the city agency in charge of enforcing parking regulations. The fox, in other words, is still in the hen house.

A day may be coming, however, when clicking the orange "submit" button on a web site or mobile application like UncivilServants.org does more than just slap a virtual summons on an illegally parked car. During the 2011 New York City Council hearings on parking placard bar codes, Jonathan Kalkin, a former chair of the Roosevelt Island Operating Corporation Operations Committee, suggested that citizens could do parking enforcement on their own by being "able to scan, get that information and then upload it as a complaint to 311," New York City's government hotline. Crowd-sourced parking enforcement would remove NYPD traffic enforcement agents from the difficult position of having to ticket and tow their colleagues. It would "stop police officers from worrying about protecting their own," Kalkin argued.

The development of effective and responsible tools to provide citizens with legal enforcement power is clearly the next frontier in crowd-sourced public accountability. The technology has arrived. Law and culture have not yet caught up.

1 http://www.villagevoice.com/2006-04-04/news/watching-the-detectives/full/

2 http://www.nytimes.com/2007/03/22/nyregion/22parking.html

3 http://www.nydailynews.com/new-york/bogus-parking-placard-advocacy-group-park-new-york-city-single-ticket-article-1.128164

The Fab City: Hard and Soft Tools for Smart Citizens' Production of the City

Tomás Diez

Introduction

Today's economic, environmental, social and political crises are the result of a model that was shaped during the last 100 years. This model is based on oil processing (energy and raw materials), chain production and the creation of a global economic system. Our oil-based economy and serialized production model have allowed humanity to increase the capacity of manufacturing resources to solve its basic needs while investing less time and fewer human resources and to furthermore generate new materials and processes for the consumption of goods and services by the masses. The spatial separation of production from consumption, and the acceleration of manufacturing processes (mainly in the food industry) enabled humans to have more time to expend on other activities. The rise of an entertainment-based society is not a causality: Once your basic needs are met, you can use the most recent technological discoveries to consume and produce spectacle and leisure. We need to change our relationship with technology in order to achieve a more sustainable, productive and knowledge-based way of living. Production has to be brought closer to consumption, and our stock has to be administrated with more efficient and demand-based dynamics.

A Place Where Everything Happens, or Used to Happen: The City

In today's society, most human interaction takes place in cities. Urban settlements are among the most complex systems created by mankind, and are the places where the biggest challenges of our future will happen. It is a fact that our present productive model is putting the sustainability of the next generations at risk; it might sound like a '70s or late-90s assertion, but the sentiment remains and is becoming even more critical, and from different points of view as well. The technology, the resources and the administrative make-up of cities today are obsolete and, in the main, continue to be based on outdated models that encompass economic, social, political, environmental and technological perspectives. The majority of our cities function under an old, industrialized model that emerged around 200 years ago in Manchester and Liverpool. That industrialized model relied upon access to raw materials and cheap physical labor, and allowed the growth of certain countries, such as those we know today as the G7 or, most recently, Asian giants exemplified by China. Today, our western societies consume food and products manufactured thousands of kilometers away from cities; they produce trash, and speculate with money and resources that sometimes do not even exist.

As previously stated, the economic and productive model shaped the industrialized city, firstly by establishing centers of production within the city borders, then by absorbing the population of rural areas. People came to live in precarious conditions, but were attracted by the new possibilities of urbanization. Later on, production left the cities and moved thousands of kilometers away from the urban centers, increasing the use of fossil fuels to transport goods, leveling down job opportunities and, more critically, separating knowledge of production from consumption. The result: Cities act as big trash factories and are dependent on technology produced far away. Our cities manifest the consumption-based model we are living today.

However, cities need technology to function and to offer their citizens the commodities to live and to satisfy their needs. The basic logistics of urban centers are dependent on a core technological capacity; this allows them to provide services, facilitate resource distribution and resolve emergencies within their limits. But the cities of today not only have to fulfill the needs of its citizens through the construction of large infrastructures such as pipelines, fiber optic networks, public transportation or high quality public spaces. Today's cities need to innovate and create their own technologies, and to share them with other urban centers in order to construct solutions for the city, by the city, and through its citizens.

Where Is Technology Produced? Why?

In the Medieval city, most of the productive activity happened within the city walls, which created the physical boundaries for knowledge exchange. The city walls served as a physical limit, which concentrated its problems but also forged solutions through the local production of goods. In this sense, we can say that artisan craftwork was produced in order to satisfy a local need or desire which could then be connected with other towns or cities in a secondary level of importance. The industrialization of production decoupled the purpose of fabrication from its immediate reality; it scaled up into regional, national and global interests and, furthermore, into a standardized production system that finally created what we observe today: A person in Delhi uses the same microprocessor in his/her computer as a person in Buenos Aires, Cape Town or Washington. But at the same time we do not need to use the same cups, tables, toys or specific tools in China, the Ukraine or Peru. This might not be important in the case of a functional item, but it becomes serious when it refers to the public lighting of a city, a public transportation system, or the furniture we use in our living rooms. Most of these objects were conceived and produced for the environmental conditions and users of faraway places and are removed from the reality of those who own and use them. More critically: These objects and devices have been unified or simplified to gain a foothold with differing peoples, in different countries, with different conditions, thus creating an average global standard set for consumption. A universal consumption kit.

A recent history of why we use what we use: If we go back to the last century, we will find out that a large amount of the technology we consume today has been developed in the military industry; this is what allowed us to create most of the inventions that define our everyday life: from how and what we eat, to the way we communicate with each other, among many other simple activities. In *Sex, Bombs and Burgers,* Peter Nowak states:

"We've come to the point where it's almost impossible to separate any American-created technology from the American military. Chances are, the military has had a hand in it, and industry has been a willing partner" (2010, p. 12).

From Nowak's book we can understand that besides the war industry, it is mainly the most basic instincts of human nature that have instigated the development of today's major technological advances; the food industry and the sex industry have created major changes in our everyday life, in ways most of us are not aware of. The First and Second World Wars gave us everyday items like the microwave oven, the handheld camera or personal computers. Later on, the Cold War spawned today's Internet when Vint Cerf and his colleagues conceptualized a distributed network of connected nodes in order to maintain the information flow in case of a nuclear attack on the US. Today, the Internet has turned out to be the most influential recent invention shaping the way we live, share and produce.

"Internet has changed our lives, but has not changed our cities" (Guallart, 2012, p. 9). In his recent book, *La ciudad autosuficiente (The Self-Sufficient City)*, Vicente Guallart, the Chief Architect of the City of Barcelona, develops a whole conceptual framework on how a multi-scalar approach, mainly supported by the intersection between information and communication technology (ICT), urbanism and ecology, will reshape the model of our cities, just like it did a hundred years ago with the oil industry, or with serialized production.

"The information society, however, connects people to people, objects including buildings with buildings, including community so that the flow of resources between nodes occurs on a smaller scale, allowing, from the interaction of thousands of similar nodes, the <<emergent>> system" (Guallart, 2012, p. 55).

The industrialized model seems to be under stress, and we are certainly at a moment of transition through the creation of new tools that will redefine and shape our reality. The informational and productive tools in the hands of citizens seem to be the key players in this process, explained in *The Self-Sufficient City*:

"The regeneration of cities on the model of connected self-sufficiency only makes sense if it allows people to have more control over their lives and gives them more power, as part of a social network" (p. 55).

There is no question about the rise of new tools for citizen-based accountability, from the common tools such as community radio or printed advertisement to the most recent Kickstarter projects like Twine (http://supermechanical.com/twine/), Ninja Blocks (http://ninjablocks.com/) or Air Quality Egg (http://airqualityegg.com/). We certainly agree that ICT is putting into the hands of people a vast access to new ways of participation in everyday life decisions. Radio, video reporting, blogging, environmental sensing ... today, as citizens, we can gain access to open source tools and platforms, and use them to denounce irregularities and crime, share an event, create a new voice in our neighborhood, or communicate with our community. The case of a nine-year-old pupil in the UK was one of the media trends in 2012; she took pictures of her school's food and shared it on her own blog, creating awareness of the condition of kids' nutrition. From the *Daily Mail* website:

"Martha Payne, aged nine, uploaded a picture of her lunch. Martha's blog soon began to fill with pictures and reviews on the food of her school, which attracted the attention of mass audiences" (William Cook, *Daily Mail Online*, 2 Oct. 2012).

Martha's case is fascinating; she just used a digital camera (or the one from her smartphone) and uploaded to an existing blogging platform. Now Martha is a celebrity and runs a charity program for children in Malawi. This might have been extremely enhanced by the media and our spectator society, but at the same time it makes us think about the possibilities of the tools we have in our hands today, and how significant they could be if we turn them into means to improve our living conditions.

Beyond the existing tools in the form of websites, apps, and other traditional tools, today's citizen participation in accountability could be exponentially changed by the introduction of "the tools to make the tools."

The Productive City — Barcelona 5.0

Our cities import products and produce trash — tons of it: obsolete products, plastic packaging, cans and rotten food that end up in our trash bins, most of it never to be re-used again. According to an Institution of Mechanical Engineers report published in January 2013, 1.2 to 2 billion metric tons of food produced annually in the world never gets eaten; in the meantime 870 million people are undernourished. Barcelona is one of these cities wanting to change that. Imagine productive neighborhoods equipped with digital fabrication laboratories (Fab Labs) and connected with other neighborhoods and cities in the world, exchanging knowledge and addressing the problems of the community, like public lightning, playgrounds, environmental conditions, energy production, food production, or even local production of needed goods such as domestic furniture or simple mobility systems; using old products as raw materials, recycling plastic to be 3-D-printed again, or using old electronics to produce new, useful devices. Futuristic?

Fab Labs were initially created by the Center for Bits and Atoms (CBA) at the Massachusetts Institute of Technology. Their success was surprising even to their creators; as Director Neil Gershenfeld informally states at conferences: "They happened by accident." Fab Labs started as a kit of tools and machines that CBA provided to a local community in the inner city of Boston as part of its outreach program. Fab Labs started to spread in Ghana, Norway and India in the early 2000s, and then in Barcelona, Amsterdam and the rest of the world. Today there are around 150 labs in more than 35 countries, on all continents. All Fab Labs share the same inventory of machines and processes, and are connected through the Internet and video conferences, building one of the biggest networks and communities of makers in the world.

Fab Labs have a global scale, but Barcelona is forging a new model of a productive city that is based on local manufacturing enabled by the use of digital fabrication machines and processes, and more importantly: by the construction of a makers' community not only limited to Fab Labs. Antoni Vives (Deputy Major of Barcelona) and Vicente Guallart (Chief Architect of Barcelona) launched the Fab City project at the seventh Fab Lab Conference in 2011, which took place in Lima, Peru. The Fab City project resulted from a discussion that happened in Boston between Vives, Guallart and Neil Gershenfeld. The discussion was basically centered on the question of productivity in cities, and how our cities today only import goods and produce trash. Guallart informally named this model "From PITO to DIDO" (PITO refers to "product in, trash out"; DIDO refers to "data in, data out"). Barcelona is proposing a new model for cities, based on production within the city, recycling materials and satisfying local needs by local invention. This would be the DIDO model, in which the majority of the imports and exports of a city happen in terms of bytes (information), and all the atoms are handled on the local scale. This is the Fab City project: productive citizens using common tools and sharing knowledge about making and manufacturing to solve local needs, generate new businesses and educational programs; a whole productive city.

This year, Fab City's plans include the opening of two new Fab Labs in inner Barcelona: one in the district of Les Corts, one of the city's most wealthy neighborhoods with a highly educated population and access to commodities; the other in one of the most conflictive districts: Nou Barris, located on the city's periphery, based on a 1960s urban development model, superblocks with a great amount of challenges to tackle and high rates of youth unemployment. Both Fab Labs will be equipped with the basic machines and tools that each Fab Lab has network-wide; it will be named: "Ateneus de Fabricació," a Catalan translation of "Fabrication Athenaeum." These two Fab Labs will be the beginning of a city network, with the objective of installing at least one Athenaeum per district in the coming years. The idea of the Fab Labs in the city is basically to provide the means and tools for the citizens to incubate business, learn new ways of production and fabricate change for their communities, in strong connection with the worldwide network of makers.

The Institute for Advance Architecture of Catalonia (IAAC) and Fab Lab Barcelona have developed projects that could be implemented on the scale of a microcontroller for an entire house, like the Fab Lab House, constructed in 2010 for the Solar Decathlon Europe competition, or on the scale of a city or territory. The Fab City is a city-scale project that will be strongly supported by other projects developed within IAAC and the Fab Lab Barcelona: Valldaura Self-Sufficient Labs, which exist on a territorial scale. Valldaura is a 130-hectare estate located 15 minutes from the Barcelona city center inside the Collserola Metropolitan Park, the green center of the metropolitan area. Valldaura was acquired by IAAC in 2010, and aims to develop different kinds of programs focusing on the three main principles of self-sufficiency: the production of energy, the production of goods and the production of food. Valldaura will be the incubator of new ways of production using natural and sustainable processes, and of the generation of new materials. It will allow for field tests and the development of solutions for the self-sufficient city in an old monastery (Can Valldaura) which, at the same time, is connected with the world.

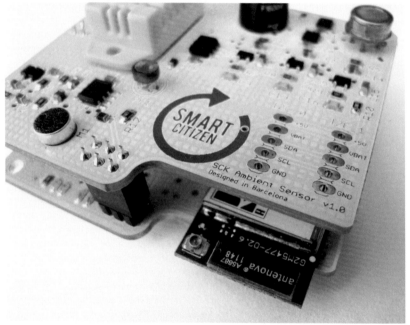

Smart Citizen Kit. Developed by the Smart Citizen team: Alex Posada, Miguel de Heras, Guillem Camprodon, and Tomás Diez, 2012

Do It Yourself Is Not New, Do It with Others Is Better

The Whole Earth Catalogue was published by Stewart Brand between 1968 and 1998 as a DIY guide for making and providing access to tools for people to develop a more self-sustainable way of living. Each issue of the catalogue was updated with inventions and how-to guides to build different devices such as water filters, solar-powered lights and other tools and objects to not only improve individual life, but community living as well. What happened to all these movements? Why did the catalogue decrease its editions in the early 1970s and finally cease publication in 1998? The catalogue became obsolete, maybe because it was not needed in a consumer-based world.

Even though the DIY movement was far from dead after the *Whole Earth Catalogue* disappeared, DIY is experiencing a new impulse today through the use of Internet and open source tools such as Instructables (http://www.instructables.com/), Makezine (http://makezine.com/), or Thingiverse (http://www.thingiverse.com/). These platforms, among others, are giving people access to new tools of creation and production, not only by providing instructions on how to make anything from a solar-powered light to a complete 3-D printer, but by allowing users to upload, edit and share those instructions and knowledge on how to make things. If we link these platforms with Fab Labs (http://fab.cba.mit.edu/about/faq/), MakerSpaces (http://makerspace.com/), HackerSpaces (http://hackerspaces.org/wiki/) and other facilities for local manufacturing, then we will have a perfect mixture of the global-digital world and the local-physical one, both articulated and synchronized in order to produce solutions and satisfy needs and desires, hopefully without compromising others.

The Smart Citizen

During the past few years in Barcelona, the term "Smart City" has been in most of the mainstream forums, meetings and events, mainly related to technology, urbanism and architecture. Barcelona hosts one of the most important Smart Cities forums in the world: The Smart City Expo, which brings the biggest companies (IBM, CISCO, ABERTIS, etc.) and important decision makers of city governments from different countries to the city every year to discuss the new role of ICT in the development of more optimized and efficient cities. The forum is a perfect marketplace, and the term "Smart City" is the perfect brand to buy and sell new products related to technology and cities. But where is the citizen in this whole ecosystem of big trades, infrastructure investment and new urban plans?

Together with a group of fellow researchers at IAAC, Fab Lab Barcelona and MID (Media Interactive Design studio), we began raising questions to ourselves and to our students about the role of the citizen in the production of information of the city. At IAAC we run a complete studio class on Smart Cities and the role of ICT in new urbanism. One of the main questions is: Which tools do we have as citizens to produce information or goods in the city? In order to answer those questions ourselves, we started by developing an Arduino-based kit that allows a user to capture data from the environment, which can inform us about the levels of air quality, noise, temperature, humidity, light, solar radiation or radio wave exposure, and can automatically upload the data to an online platform (http://www.smartcitizen.me) to share and compare. The kit uses any domestic WiFi connection, is powered by a lithium battery and, once connected, will automatically start to transmit data to a server in order to share it with others. The Smart Citizen project was launched in a crowd-funding campaign using a Barcelona-based platform Goteo (http://www.goteo.org) that mainly supports open source projects. In September 2012 the Smart Citizen project achieved its campaign goal, raising 13,748 Euros within 80 days to produce the first 200 kits and develop the first version of the online platform. Data from the kits will be displayed on the platform and be available for users to share, create visualizations, or generate triggers. This was ultimately developed to provide more tools for interaction between the citizen and the city.

The Smart Citizen project aims to develop a local network of data collectors not only in Barcelona, but also in other cities of the world. Besides the fact that there are several projects similar to Smart Citizen mentioned before, one of its strengths is the "localization" of the data, and the creation of a local community. The aim of the Smart

Citizen project is better explained through this metaphor: Make the cloud (referring to the amount of online information and data) "rain" in front of our homes, and use hardware and software tools to act in the city to understand it.

Smart Citizen online platform,http://www.smartcitizen.me. Developed by the Smart Citizen team: Alexandre Dubor, Guillem Camprodon, Gabriel Bello Diaz, and Tomás Diez, 2012

A New Literacy

The introduction of new tools and technology in our everyday lives has shaped the way we learn and what we learn. Until the 1960s, most office work was done without computers; course materials in universities were printed; medium-sized business did their bookkeeping using folders stored on shelves. In the 1970s, computers became accessible to small and medium-sized businesses and organizations, requiring new skills for new tasks to perform with those new tools. Finally, in the 1980s, computers became accessible to anyone; the popularization of personal computers (PCs) reached our homes. In the early 1990s, most of the schools in the Western World introduced computers into classrooms and libraries, and learning how to use word processors or image treatment software became part of standard educational programs. Today's global operations depend on those new skills acquired by the new workers, leaving the machines in the factory, and moving to offices in tall buildings in the city. As most of us know, this model of employees working in front of a computer in crowded worked spaces is likely obsolete; the 2008 crisis was merely a starting point of a probable huge collapse. More and more office workers are being made redundant, and it seems that even those skills are not up-to-date anymore.

The "first work, then rest" model seems to be obsolete, as well the "time = money" equation we use to quantify and qualify what we do, how, and when. Today, most of the world's unemployed have time to spend, but not the money to accompany it; the failure of the system resides in the fact that "nothing moves without money." This is a pathology that needs to be healed by the will of the citizens. The Internet enables us to have access to high-quality courses in computer science, neurology, physics and electronics (i.e., EdX courses offered by MIT, Stanford and Harvard), or simple tutorials on how to edit a movie, how to edit pictures using Photoshop, how to program in C or Python (Codecademy, Kahn Academy). Learning is no longer related to a formal institution, it can be achieved by anyone, anywhere, anytime and for free. Just like we learn how to use Word, Excel or PowerPoint, we will learn how to model in 3-D, operate a laser cutter, or program a microcontroller. These new skills will determine our power to influence how our reality is shaped, because we will have access to the tools to do so.

Recently, a media series focused on the importance of learning programming, or coding, and according to the BBC, coding could be compared to learning Latin 2000 years ago. Moreover, learning code is basically shaping a new way of thinking:

"That, really, is what it means to inhabit the coded world: to understand what it means to use these machines to think with. This is what thinking has become in the 21st century condition" (Tom Armitage, *BBC Online*, 26 Dec. 2012).

Not only coding, but modeling and scanning software and tools, or any other skill that will allow us to relate the physical and the digital worlds, will become mandatory in any other course at schools, universities and training programs.

The Next Five Years

"A once-shuttered warehouse is now a state-of-the art lab where new workers are mastering the 3D printing that has the potential to revolutionize the way we make almost everything" (Barack Obama, President of the United States of America, during the State of the Union Address. Quoted by Doug Gross on *CNN Tech*, online edition, 13 Feb. 2013).

President Obama is referring to 3-D printing as the major boost in today's production model, but might be too simplistic. 3-D printing is the tip of the iceberg; distributed and personal manufacturing is much more complex in essence, and at the same time it might take several years to print fully functional objects. Neil Gershenfeld states in his most recent article in *Foreign Affairs* magazine ("How to Make Almost Anything" November/December 2012) that the 3-D printing fever could be compared with the coverage in media that the microwave had in the 1950s, considered as the replacement of the kitchen. It is proven that the microwave made our lives better, but we still need the rest of the tools in a kitchen to make complex food. Fab Labs could be compared with that kitchen, and 3-D printers with microwaves. Instead of food, new inventions are being produced in those labs, at a faster speed than industry and university are doing today.

3-D printing might not change the world itself, but it is the trigger for a major movement we will be part of. It seems that there is a historical cycle, and the artisans, DIYers or the guilds are finding new tools and media to make, collaborate and produce technology. With the tools, conditions and reality we are living in and occupying today, the human factor is the only aspect that seems to remain constant. Most of the phenomena we are talking about today were part of a previous period in the human condition. What is really changing are the means to achieve these processes, as well as how we can now link things that previously seemed incompatible into a simple point of view.

The upcoming years will be transitional and critical for the construction of what will probably be called the "Second Renaissance" or "High-Tech Medieval Age."

References

Armitage, Tom (2012). "Viewpoint: Computer Code Frees Us to Think in New Ways." *BBC Online*, 26 Dec. Web. 18 Feb. 2013.

Cook, William (2012). "Malawi one, Scotland nil! Girl, 9, who was banned from blogging about disgusting school dinners gives thumbs up to breakfast as she visits African children." *Daily Mail Online*, 2 Oct. Web. 18 Feb. 2013.

Gershenfeld, Neil (2005). *Fab: The Coming Revolution on Your Desktop—From Personal Computers to Personal Fabrication*. New York: Basic Books.

Gershenfeld, Neil (2012). "How to Make Almost Anything." *Foreign Affairs*, November/December. Web. 18 Feb. 2013.

Gross, Doug (2013). "Obama's speech highlights rise of 3-D printing." *CNN Tech*, 13 Feb. 2013. Web. 2013.

Guallart, Vicente (2012). *La ciudad autosuficiente: Habitar en la sociedad de la información*. Barcelona: RBA Libros.

Mitchell, William J. (2003). *Me++: The Cyborg Self and the Networked City*. Cambridge, MA: The MIT Press.

Nowak, Peter (2010). *Sex, Bombs and Burgers: How War, Porn and Fast Food Created Technology As We Know It*. Toronto: Viking Canada.

Rifkin, Jeremy (1995). *The End of Work: The Decline of the Global Labor Force and the Dawn of the Post-Market Era*. New York: G.P. Putnam's Sons.

Tapscott, Don and Williams, Anthony D. (2008). *Wikinomics: How Mass Collaboration Changes Everything*. New York: Penguin USA.

Martha Payne's blog: http://neverseconds.blogspot.co.at/

All images are copyrighted by IAAC and Fab Lab Barcelona.

Text revised by Jonathan Minchin.

Answers from Within

Katja Schechtner

In this essay, I will argue that the effectiveness of accountability technologies ultimately depends on the level of cooperation between the citizen and her government. The cooperative relationship itself depends first on willing individual actors within the addressed institutions to listen, answer and instigate change. Secondly, the institutions have to create an internal culture that supports those internal champions. Finally, they have to adapt their organizational mechanism to the new forms of information exchange and interaction that are demanded by the public.

As Leonardo Bonanni describes in his article included in this volume, internal agents of change are "employees who advocate for a change from within." They play an important role in integrating bottom-up information with top-down administration and management. Champions for change from within, such as Deputy Inspector Gin Yee of New York City, who responded to public requests to enforce parking laws also for city officials, or the Berlin government official who spearheaded open data projects by inviting an applied research institute, Fraunhofer FOKUS, to help formulate an open data strategy, act as driving forces that initiate new forms of collaboration between public know-how and organizational expertise.

Although those internal activists still face uphill battles within many reluctant governments and businesses, a growing number of politicians, civil servants and corporate leaders actively embrace and shape new technologies and models to better integrate the knowledge of their citizens and customers.

Initially juxtaposing top-down government with bottom-up knowledge, James C. Scott, in *Seeing Like a State*,[1] argues for such a new, mediated form of governmental planning. He calls for an administration that continuously engages citizens in adapting and changing the policies and practices that govern the land, thus breaking the one-dimensional script of the repressive state at the top and the oppressed at the bottom: "An institution, social form, or enterprise that takes much of its shape from the evolving metis"[2] of the people engaged in it will thereby enhance their range of experience and skills. Following the advice of the saying "use it or lose it," the "metis-friendly institution both uses and renews a valuable public good."[3]

Accountability technologies are concerned with supporting the creation and application of this public good: by employing new, technologically-mediated forms of collecting, documenting and visualizing the collective metis—practical, experiential, local and informal knowledge—and finally helping to find the right addressee for the generated information.

Their potential to serve citizens and institutions has been acknowledged by different multilateral, national and municipal organizations, but typically institutions are still grappling with questions pertaining to opening up their data to a wider public. While the Freedom of Information Act is a guideline for public institutions in the US to publish their data, questions pertaining to sharing data with the public still remain under debate. The reluctance to share encompasses all fields—ranging from infrastructure and environmental data, to economic statistics, and even information about complaints filed by the public.

Whereas this organizational indecisiveness has brought forward a lot of grassroots accountability initiatives willing to fight uphill battles, the first results of a growing understanding that new technologies can be employed to offer better services to the citizens are noticeable at various multilateral, national and municipal levels.

As UK Cabinet Office Minister Francis Maude stated in 2012: "The transparency movement has opened a Pandora's box. It's transforming the world for the better. And now we have started, there's just no going back. But why would you want to stop transparency, even if you could? Open data is driving growth and prosperity. Data is the raw material of the 21st century and a resource for a new generation of entrepreneurs. But transparency is not just about economics. Transparency shines light on underperformance and inefficiencies in public services. It allows citizens and the media to hold governments to account, strengthening civil society and building more open societies."[4]

Addressing similar concerns, an international multilateral initiative to stimulate open government was started by a cooperation of nine civil society institutions and government representatives from eight countries on four continents: Brazil, Indonesia, Mexico, Norway, the Philippines, South Africa, the UK and the USA. Until 2013, about 50 more governments joined this Open Government Partnership (OGP). Understanding that citizen initiatives must find knowledgeable counterparts within the governments, OGP member countries commit to increase access to new technologies for openness and accountability, and among other things call for the "use of technological innovations by government employees and citizens alike."[5] Several initiatives, e.g., the Apps for Asia[6] or the mycity[7] app program, are currently working on new models to bring public administrators and citizens together with tech developers to address issues ranging from lacking walkability to helping local governments turn civic inquiries into tangible community improvements.

The first step of many such projects: Releasing data sets to the public, who will eventually use their analytic skills to hold governments or companies accountable based on exactly the information they were freely given before, has already not been welcomed by many experts within the different organizations. The next step: Actively involving citizens and consumers in the redesign of policies and services will be even more disruptive. While governments and businesses in the past have learned to deal with public sentiments and have established procedures to let people voice their feelings, they are challenged by the idea of citizen experts who, beyond voicing their perceptions, are able to prove their observations based on data. To embrace the notion that even their status as experts with superior domain knowledge can and will now be challenged by the "amateurs united," armed with new tools and models of collaboration and information collaboration, is an even bigger step for institutions and the many individuals that form them.

On a multilateral level, this initial pushback by experts who felt challenged in their own domain was experienced by Patrick Meier and his volunteer group when they were building crisis maps for Haiti (see p.104ff). But he also describes how quickly the UN—guided by some of its highest officials—started to work with them. On national and municipal levels, small units have been also created within the larger governmental institutions to act as interfaces with the tech-savvy public. These labs range from governmental units as design thinking labs, to publicly funded co-creation spaces, to small new technology groups within established urban planning units.

International examples are the Boston New Urban Mechanics in the US,[8] the Mind-Lab in Denmark,[9] Fab Lab Barcelona in Spain,[10] the Open Government Data Lab in Vienna, Austria,[11] the design innovation unit of SPRING Singapore,[12] or the Pulse Lab in Jakarta, Indonesia.[13] True to the spirit of the cities they were founded in, they stress different aspects of interfacing with the citizens. Some are fostering the entrepreneurial spirit in the design of technologies and services for more efficient government. Others see it as a link to incorporate the interests of their younger population into new e-government services. And others again see it as a logical extension to their already established public participation practices. However, all centers act as education platforms about the potentials and challenges of the digital technologies for politicians, governmental employees and citizens.

Christian Bason describes three shared challenges for design-led innovation in government that also apply more broadly to any form of technology, innovation and public participation units: creating authorizing environments; building and accessing capacity; and opening up bureaucracy to co-production.[14]

Creating authorizing environments relates to the need for embedding the new structures as a legitimate part of the policy-making infrastructure. Building and accessing capacity and opening up bureaucracy address the need for institutional procedures for finding and integrating external experts with backgrounds related to holistic city management, rather than single, sector-focused consultants.

With respect to accountability technologies—whose developers and users are, to a large extent, motivated by governmental failures or omissions—a fourth challenge needs to be met: How to interact with the government if the data presented conflicts with the political will?

While in many ways it is too early to fully understand how accountability technologies can help to create new pathways for solving those conflicts, they add three aspects to this effort: First, in case of severe political unrest, they can help to monitor the actions of both parties, which has been extensively described in relation to the Arab spring and is again demonstrated during the protests at Gezi Park in Istanbul, Turkey.[15] Secondly, within regular democratic governing procedures, accountability technologies level the playing field with regard to information. And thirdly, by their very nature—data-based information interpretation—they adopt the traditional discussion and decision patterns of administrations, thus making it easier for governments to find new answers and new ways to answer "from within."

1   James C. Scott (1998), *Seeing Like a State: How Certain Schemes to Improve the Human Condition Have Failed*, The Yale ISPS Series (New Haven, CT and London: Yale University Press).

2   Metis, a word of Greek origin, is translated by Scott as "the knowledge that can only come from practical experience."

3   Scott, p. 356.

4   Francis Maude, "Transparency brings tangible benefits," *The Guardian*, 26 Sep. 2012. Available at http://www.guardian.co.uk/public-leaders-network/2012/sep/26/francis-maude-open-government-partnership?INTCMP=SRCH. Last retrieved on 27 May 2013.

5   Open Government Declaration, Sep. 2011. Available at http://www.opengovpartnership.org/open-government-declaration. Last retrieved on 27 May 2013.

6   http://www.adb.org/news/apps-asia-winners-featured-adb-annual-meeting

7   http://appmycity.org/

8   http://www.newurbanmechanics.org/

9   http://www.newurbanmechanics.org/

10 http://fablabbcn.org/

11 http://data.wien.gv.at/

12 http://www.designsingapore.org/

13 http://www.unglobalpulse.org/pulse-lab/jakarta

14 Christian Bason (2013), "Design-Led Innovation in Government," *Stanford Social Innovation Review*, Spring 2013, p. 17.

15 http://themonkeycage.org/2013/06/03/twitter-and-the-turkish-protests-post-weekend-update/

Crowdsourcing Situational Awareness

Interview with Patrick Meier

In your work, you focus on situations where the right information at the right place and time can decide over the life and well-being of many people. You were formative for the emerging field of crisis mapping and did extensive research on the role of social media in anti-government protests. How would you describe/characterize your field and its central goals?

I guess my interest evolved over time. In terms of the connection to crisis mapping and digital activism, the common thread really is technology and situational awareness. The idea of being able to use new technologies to get a better sense of what is happening, where it is happening, and to whom it is happening and so on. These crisis maps are one way to provide individuals with an at-a-glance understanding as to what is unfolding in a particular situation or a particular crisis or revolution. There are lots of commonalities in this sense in the crisis mapping space, in the digital humanitarian space: Humanitarian organizations and digital volunteer groups use crisis mapping to provide humanitarian organizations with situational awareness they need to make better decisions in terms of how they respond to disasters and how to prioritize the disaster response and so on. In the context of digital activism, you can use crisis mapping technologies to document repressive activity, human rights violations, brutality, threats against journalists, and so on and so forth. And again, the idea is to surface this information, to make it more visible to a wider audience. There are very interesting overlaps—the Ushahidi platform,[1] for example, has been used both for digital activism, election monitoring and disaster response. Other commonalities I have gotten increasingly interested in is when you see a cross-over: When you see, for example, that technology-savvy activists in Iran, having used Twitter and other technologies as a part of their activism, are using some of these same technologies and networks again for disaster response. This is really interesting because we see that social capital gets generated when you start collaborating. Collective action is a result of pre-existing social capital, but collective action projects and exercises can also help catalyze or nurture digital social capital. When social capital is built up in the context of a political crisis, we see added value because the same networks and the same social capital are used again in the context of an earthquake or a flood and so on ... and vice versa.[2]

This point that you raise about social capital is very interesting—when we look at traditional volunteer organizations that operate in physical space, strong connections between the individual volunteers are obviously important, but when we look at digital communities, let's say Wikipedia editors, then it seems until recently that the emphasis was more on intellectual capital, on learning, sharing information, while the social bonds are much weaker and less important. How would you see the forms of social capital that you've just mentioned?

This goes back to the whole argument that Malcolm Gladwell set off a couple of years back,[3] where he was basically saying social media is not conducive to developing strong social bonds, but only weak bonds. But what you need for civil existence are strong bonds, trusted networks. I think there has been enough pushback and compelling arguments to show that it is not an either/or—that you need a combination of strong and weak ties for digital activism—civil resistance and non-violent action. I think this applies as well to disaster response, although when we are talking about digital humanitarian response, there is really no off-line component in the same way there is the off-line in digital activism and civil resistance. The advantage of the digital humanitarian response is that these ties ... I can only speak from personal experience, but I think I have developed very strong personal ties through the work that we have done with the Standby Volunteer Task Force,[4] this global network of about 900 volunteers in 80 different countries. I have gotten to know people and worked with them in such difficult and stressful situations over extended periods of time, day and night, that you spend more time with them than anyone else around you, because you have got a major disaster at hand. And so you work day and night with these people around the world, and you become very strongly connected with them. I just recently met one of the core team members of the Standby Task Force in person for the first time a couple of months ago. We have never met each other in the past three years, but we are going to be friends for life now just because of everything we have gone through together—I consider that a very strong bond.

So I think that social media can actually be a source of social capital in ways that haven't even been explored as much in the literature. In fact, I have seen very little rigorous and even non-rigorous academic research trying to understand this linkage of social media to social capital.

In this volume we also have examples of initiatives such as GuttenPlag, where all participants were anonymous, and knew each other only through pseudonyms. It is a very interesting question under which circumstances social capital serves a purpose, is necessary, or is something that is only relevant in a specific project context, but not in others ... To what degree can we generalize these mechanisms?

I would be hesitant to generalize too much. As far as traditional social capital that is catalyzed without online social networks in a context of disaster response, this new book by Daniel Aldrich[5] provides a very compelling mixed-methods research approach to demonstrate that social capital is not just a myth. He does a really rigorous job in showing the difference that social capital can make, but he is also very upfront about saying that we should not romanticize social capital. Because what social capital ultimately does is facilitate collective action over common and shared goals, but now these common and shared goals could be against human rights—if you look at extremist groups, that's social capital, and they are very good at collective action. So I would not want to romanticize it either, but what we need is more research to better understand especially the online component of social capital.

Let me put your efforts into a larger historical context: In what ways are the current forms of collective action different from past forms of civic activism, including the civil rights ('50s-'60s), environmental ('70s), or environmental justice ('80s) movements? Apart from the facilitation of situational awareness, are there other things that social media brings to the table? What is the role and significance of technology?

It is this idea of self-organization that I think is also really interesting—that these platforms are not just for communication, but also for self-organization, especially if you look at how some of these crisis mapping platforms have been used to crowdsource not only problems, but solutions as well. These are not just maps; they become platforms for self-organization: when you start matching needs with existing resources. In the context of disaster response, like we saw in Russia during 2010 with the massive fires, where volunteer groups set up this crisis map to match resources and create this self-organized, mutual aid approach that I think is incredibly compelling. We can see this as well in civil resistance and digital activism. So this idea of self-organization, these platforms that can match very locally, at the hyper-local level, needs and resources in a very horizontal, rather than hierarchical way, can be quite powerful, especially in areas of limited statehood.

You mentioned institutions and how you bypass them. This raises the question: How do you make the data actionable? Can you tell us more about your interface with existing structures and institutions? Based on your work, can you comment on the challenges you encountered in this regard, and talk about some of the strategies for addressing these challenges?

This is something that has been intriguing me for a long time. When we did the disaster response in Haiti in January 2010 and people were saying, "This is the most up-to date, comprehensive crisis map available to the humanitarian community" and we got a lot of publicity, that created a lot of tension with humanitarians. And some of it is warranted I have to say, we had way too much publicity, completely overblown. And at the same time, unfortunately, the UN really messed up their response to Haiti. This is not just me saying this; the former head of UN OHA[6] sent a highly critical e-mail that was then leaked to the media, where he basically said, "This was a complete disaster in terms of our response." So, that did not help, and the fact that they had a bunch of volunteers in snowy Boston, who were not humanitarians, had never done humanitarian response and who had never left Boston, but were still able to provide the kind of situational awareness faster and in ways that were more useable, created a lot of tension between us, the digital humanitarian community and the established humanitarian community, for many months. And it was only at the end of that year that a dialog began to happen. In October of that year, I happened to be at a Mashable Conference, on a panel with a senior level UN official. Before the panel we talked, and he basically said—"Listen, you are clearly not going to go away, so we have decided to take a constructive engagement approach. Let's find out how we can work together." Shortly after that conversation, the UN and OHA got in touch with us. A lot of what we did, and I am not saying this in a patronizing way, was educational, since a lot of professional humanitarians still don't understand what we do. And we learn from them, the professionals, so we have come a long way. And then more important than Haiti was the Libya crisis map in February, March and April of 2011, which was really the first time that the UN OHA came to us and officially asked us to create a live crisis map based on social media. The fact that this happened so quickly after Haiti—I thought this would not happen for several more years—I had hope as far as the UN was concerned, because they were so open to experimenting, taking risks. Haiti showed the potential, but Libya cemented it, and was a huge win. We increasingly gained allies in the established organizations, and our success gave them leverage internally within their organizations. The Standby Task Force has been used now in 26 deployments, most of them official humanitarian deployments, over the past 26 months and our track record is impeccable. At the same time we see from the higher-ups, from Ban Ki Moon to Valerie Ames, the General Secretary for Humanitarian Affairs, very public expressions of interest and support for the use of new technologies and working with volunteer groups. OHA was integral to the launch of the digital humanitarian network, which is a network of different volunteer groups like the Standby Task Force and the Humanitarian OpenStreetMap Team, the interface between the established, professional, hierarchical, traditional humanitarian community and these very new, decentralized, highly skilled, agile, tech-savvy volunteer networks.

And do you think this cooperation between top-down and bottom-up is something we will be seeing more often in the future? What is crucial for their success over an extended period of time?

We are talking about innovation and resistance to innovation.[7] Do we see an increase in the number of these different interfaces? And then what are the early best practices for developing and sustaining them? On the first side, I think yes—if you take a step back and abstract a bit, you could describe this digital humanitarian space as an example of citizen science—and we have definitively seen a proliferation of citizen science over the past few years in so many different sectors. In fact, I have spent a lot of time interacting with citizen science projects in other sectors in order to understand what they have learned and how we can import this into our own digital humanitarian space. As far as micro-tasking or volunteer management go, there has been a lot of work in the environmental space setting up interfaces to allow volunteers to work with established environmental organizations. So we are looking at citizen science, civic engagement, which is far broader than just the humanitarian space. Something that I had not quite realized as clearly before until it was told to me by the Deputy Commissioner at the Office of the High Commissioner for Refugees (UN-HCR): When we did a project in Somalia together, he told me that this would be really great and help their operational arm, but just as important is the result that the volunteers engaged in the project will have a better understanding of what the UN-HCR does. Civic education about the goal and the mission of the UN-HCR was equally important for him as the result of the actual operational work. Now how do you go about creating interfaces that are successful? I don't know if I necessarily have the answer to that question; I can maybe just look for highlights in the humanitarian space. First, it takes a track-record; that the Standby Task Force and other groups have repeatedly proven themselves as worthy partners over a certain period of time, and publicly demonstrated the results, both good and bad. The second is allies inside the humanitarian community, who pull the strings behind the scenes, and know how to navigate the hierarchies of these institutions. It comes down to three or four individual personalities who have the credibility in these systems, and were able to make things work the way they did.

Let me go back to a very basic question — What motivates people in Boston to spend time in these initiatives at all? Now it would be easy to understand why a local group in Haiti, in Libya or Somalia would engage in collective action, but you have people sitting in Boston, D.C., or wherever, who engage in disaster relief in those places they have no obvious connection with. What is their motivation?

I think there are multiple reasons. I was as surprised as everybody else when, after a few days, hundreds of volunteers turned up to help in Haiti, and the same thing in Libya and other sites. I have different ways of explaining this. One of them is, I like to think, what makes us human is if we see others who are in need, a human reaction is that we want to help. When I saw the news of the earthquake, I wanted to do something about it, and I think this is a widely held human reaction. In the case of digital humanitarian response, you cannot help physically, but you can provide these groups with situational awareness so that they can do a better job helping people as well as possible. When we were doing the response to Haiti, one of the community leaders of the large Haitian diaspora in Boston came to visit us when we were doing this to thank us. A warm-hearted, elderly woman who told us — we have already sent money and medication to Haiti, but now you are allowing us to be a part of the actual humanitarian disaster response, you allow us to own part of this and do more than just send money. This was really one of the more highly visible examples of a diaspora which is incredibly well-placed to do this as a response.

But sometimes this is not enough. In the early days, it was enough to just send out an e-mail saying — "All right, we've got to help the UN." Now, we have to be more compelling. We spend more time explaining why this is important, what the impact is going to be, how their involvement is going to matter. I am not saying this in a bad way, but we have to market ourselves better. We have to convince our volunteers why this is worth their time, and we have to make it as easy as possible for volunteers to share their time. In digital activism, there has been this backlash against "single-click activism," and Morozov and others are saying that this is counterproductive when people think they have an impact. But that is what I want—I want it as easy as possible for volunteers to just click on buttons to help the UN, rather than making it more difficult and make them go through spreadsheets; nobody wants to work on spreadsheets ten hours in a row. So this is the design challenge. Take gamification—there are billions of hours being spent every week around the world playing computer games, so let's make it as easy and fun as playing computer games to volunteer in digital humanitarian response. At the moment, we are quite far away from that, and I am excited about a number of projects that are coming up. You can harvest all the energy through micro-tasks and channel it into one large task. The last thing I will say is that people want to learn new skills. We have a lot of professional humanitarians, who joined the Standby Task Force because you could not get this training for live crisis mapping anywhere else. We invented the workflows and procedures. And, finally, people do this because it is a good experience; they have learned something and they will put it on their CVs. So it is professional development, and I am perfectly OK with that and I am happy to write letters of recommendations for volunteers, because it is a different way of doing an internship, if you like. You are doing work with an established volunteer group that is recognized by high-level UN officials and other organizations, so we are not just clowns clowning around … we do this in a serious way. Anyway, I would have so much more to say!

1 A digital platform developed by Kenyan activists for collectively documenting incidents of violence in the aftermath of the 2008 Kenyan presidential election. See www.ushahidi.com.

2 See http://iRevolution.net/2012/08/22/civil-resistance-improve-disaster-response and http://iRevolution.net/2012/12/18/social-media-social-capital-disaster-resilience.

3 Malcolm Gladwell (2010), "Small Change - Why the Revolution Will Not Be Tweeted," *The New Yorker*, 4 October, http://www.newyorker.com/reporting/2010/10/04/101004fa_fact_gladwell?currentPage=all.

4 See http://blog.standbytaskforce.com/a-masters-thesis-on-the-motivations-behind-the-sbtf.

5 Daniel P. Aldrich (2012), *Building Resilience: Social Capital in Post-Disaster Recovery* (Chicago: University of Chicago Press).

6 The Office for Humanitarian Aid of the United Nations.

7 See http://iRevolution.net/2012/05/22/disruptive-innovation.

AUTHORS

Amber Frid-Jimenez and **Ben Dalton** are co-directors of *Data Is Political: On Contemporary Art, Design and the Politics of Information*, a research project that brings together artists, designers and data scientists in a discourse about the aesthetic and political dimensions of visualizing immense archives of digital information. Amber Frid-Jimenez is an artist, an associate profesor at Emily Carr University of Art & Design, and a principal of AFJD Studio, an interdisciplinary design firm at the intersection of architecture, information and ecology. Ben Dalton is a principal lecturer at Leeds Metropolitan University, a PhD candidate at the Royal College of Art researching new forms of digital public space in the CX Lab, and a visiting professor at the Bergen National Academy of Art & Design. They began their collective work eight years ago at the MIT Media Lab.

Leonardo Bonanni is the founder of *Sourcemap*, the platform for supply chain transparency. Companies and consumers use sourcemap.com to see where products come from, including financial, social and environmental risks. Powering the website is an enterprise social network so that—one day soon—you'll scan a product on a store shelf and be connected to those who made it. Leo is one of *Businessweek*'s "America's Most Promising Social Entrepreneurs 2012" and *Ethisphere*'s "100 Most Influential People in Business Ethics" (2011). He has a background as an architect, taught sustainable product design at Parsons and MIT, has a PhD from the MIT Media Lab, Masters' degrees from MIT and a Bachelor's from Columbia.

Tomás Diez is a Venezuela-born urbanist specialized in digital fabrication and its implications on future cities models. He is permanent faculty member at the Institute for Advanced Architecture of Catalonia (IAAC), and one of the initiators of the Fab Lab Barcelona project, which he currently directs. Co-founder of the *Smart Citizen* project and *StudioP52*, both in Barcelona. Works as a close collaborator with the Fab Foundation and the MIT Center for Bits and Atoms in the development of the Fab Lab Network worldwide. He is currently the main consultant for the Barcelona city council for the development of the "Ateneus de Fabricació (Fab Labs)" in the city.

Lawrence Lessig is the Roy L. Furman Professor of Law and Leadership at Harvard Law School, and director of the Edmond J. Safra Center for Ethics at Harvard University. Prior to rejoining the Harvard faculty, Lessig was a professor at Stanford Law School, where he founded the school's Center for Internet and Society, and at the University of Chicago. He clerked for Judge Richard Posner on the 7th Circuit Court of Appeals and Justice Antonin Scalia on the United States Supreme Court. Lessig serves on the Board of Creative Commons, MAPLight, Brave New Film Foundation, The American Academy (Berlin), AXA Research Fund and iCommons.org, and on the advisory board of the Sunlight Foundation. He is a Member of the American Academy of Arts and Sciences and the American Philosophical Association, and has received numerous awards, including the Free Software Foundation's Freedom Award, Fastcase 50 Award, and was named one of *Scientific American*'s Top 50 Visionaries. Lessig holds a BA in economics and a BS in management from the University of Pennsylvania, an MA in philosophy from Cambridge, and a JD from Yale.

Pablo Rey Mazón is a visiting scientist at the Center for Civic Media at the MIT Media Lab and the co-founder of different collectives: *Basurama* (Trash-o-rama), a multidisciplinary research group about waste, where he has developed *6000km.org*, a project that, through geotagged information, researches about the landscapes that the Spanish real estate bubble has left behind; and *Montera34*, a research group and design studio that develops organization and visualization tools like *PageOneX*, that helps understand the evolution of stories on newspaper front pages. He also takes part in several independent research groups such as: *Meipi*, which develops the open source software meipi.org for participatory mapping; *Kulturometer*, that researches about cultural expenses in the Madrid region. He holds a Master in Architecture from the Superior Technical School of Architecture of Madrid (UPM) and has also studied in the Technische Universität Dresden in Germany.

Patrick Meier is an internationally recognized thought leader on the application of new technologies for crisis early warning, humanitarian response and resilience. Presently he serves as Director of Social Innovation at the Qatar Foundation's Computing Research Institute. Previously he co-directed Harvard's Program on Crisis Mapping & Early Warning and served as Director of Crisis Mapping at Ushahidi. Patrick holds a PhD from The Fletcher School, a Pre-Doctoral Fellowship from Stanford and an MA from Columbia. He was born and raised in Africa.

Aaron Naparstek is the founder of *Streetsblog.org*, an online publication providing daily coverage of transportation, land use and environmental issues. Launched in 2006, Streetsblog has played a significant role in transforming New York City transportation policy and galvanizing a

Livable Streets movement that is pushing for a more people-centered, less automobile-oriented approach to urban planning and design in communities across North America. Currently based in Cambridge, Massachusetts, Naparstek recently completed a Loeb Fellowship at Harvard University's Graduate School of Design and is now writing, consulting and developing new projects as a Visiting Scholar at MIT's Department of Urban Studies and Planning.

Dietmar Offenhuber is a research fellow in the Senseable City Lab at the Department of Urban Studies and Planning at the Massachusetts Institute of Technology. His research focuses on accountability technologies and emerging roles of the user in urban infrastructural systems. He has led award-winning research projects investigating and improving formal and informal waste systems. He holds a Graduate Engineer Degree in Architecture from the Vienna University of Technology (2002) and a Master in Media Arts and Sciences from the MIT Media Lab (2008). He was a founding member of the Ars Electronica Futurelab in 1995, where he led the Interactive Space department as a key researcher from 2002–2004. Dietmar was a Japan Foundation Fellow at the IAMAS Institute in Gifu, Japan in 2004. From 2007–2009 he held a dual appointment as professor at the University of Art and Design Linz and key researcher at the Ludwig Boltzmann Institute for Media Art Research in Vienna.

PlagDoc is a graduate student happy to be known only by his pseudonym. PlagDoc and a friend initiated the *GuttenPlag* platform on February 17, 2011. It received the Grimme Online Award in 2011.

The Public Laboratory for Open Technology and Science (Public Lab) is a community which develops and applies open source tools to environmental exploration and investigation. By democratizing inexpensive and accessible "Do-It-Yourself" techniques, Public Lab creates a collaborative network of practitioners who actively re-imagine the human relationship with the environment. Shannon Dosemagen, Liz Barry and Matthew Lippincott are staff members of the Public Lab non-profit, and Jessi Breen and Don Blair are Public Lab organizers.

Katja Schechtner holds a dual appointment with the Asian Development Bank and the MIT Media Lab to create new strategies for large-scale urban mobility and transport technology investments and to lead research projects to integrate qualitative parameters into quantitative urban analysis tools. Furthermore she consults with the Austrian Institute of Technology AIT, where until recently she headed the Dynamic Transportation Systems group. She has a background in architecture, urban studies and technology assessment and currently focuses on understanding the potential of coupling citizens' movements with other urban utility sectors. Katja's work is stimulated by her international work experience in Asia, Africa, North America and Europe and together with fellow researchers has won a special mention at the Venice Architecture Biennale in 2012. She also serves as a curator at the Technical Museum and the Museum of Applied Arts in Vienna. Therefore, she travels extensively—and loves it.

Sarah Williams is currently an Assistant Professor of Urban Planning and the Director of the Civic Data Design Lab Project at Massachusetts Institute of Technology's (MIT) School of Architecture and Planning. The Civic Data Design Lab employs data visualization and mapping techniques to expose and communicate urban patterns and policy issues to broader audiences. Sarah's work involves translating data visualizations into policy tools and prototyping technologies for advocacy and research, using survey and census data, GPS information, maps, high- and low-res satellite imagery, analytic graphics, photographs and drawings, along with narratives and qualitative interpretations to produce images. Before coming to MIT, Williams was Co-Director of the Spatial Information Design Lab at Columbia University. Sarah has won numerous awards, including being named one of the top 25 planners in technology and a 2012 Game Changer by *Metropolis Magazine*. Her work is currently on view at the Museum of Modern Art (MoMA), New York.

Dieter Zinnbauer works for Transparency International (TI), an NGO that is present in more than 100 countries to fight corruption and promote good governance. Dieter has served as Chief Editor of the Global Corruption Report for several years, and is now coordinating TI's work on emerging policy issues and innovation. Prior to joining TI, Dieter worked as a policy analyst and research coordinator for a variety of organizations in the field of development, democratization and ICT policy, including the UN and the European Commission. On the research side, he obtained a PhD in Development Studies from the London School of Economics and Political Science, and has held several research fellowship positions, among others with the Carnegie Council on Ethics and International Affairs in New York, Oxford University, the US Social Science Research Council and the London School of Economics.

The afo architekturforum oberösterreich/this publication is subsidized by